BARRON'S
DICTIONARY
OF AMERICAN
SIGN LANGUAGE

BARRON'S
DICTIONARY
OF AMERICAN
SIGN LANGUAGE

GEOFFREY S. POOR
PROFESSOR OF ASL
NATIONAL TECHNICAL INSTITUTE FOR THE DEAF

ASL CONSULTANT & SIGNING MODEL
CHRISTINE KIM

This dictionary is dedicated to those who created and defended the stage upon which ASL grew and flourished, most prominently Lauren Clerc, Thomas Hopkins Gallaudet and his son Edward Miner Gallaudet, and George Veditz. The book is also dedicated to the National Association of the Deaf and to the many ASL teachers and researchers who have taught and illuminated this wonderful language.

About Christine Kim: Christine Kim, a deaf native signer, grew up in Orange County, California and attended University High School. She received her BS degree in Interdisciplinary Studies: Fine Arts and New Media Design from the Rochester Institute of Technology, and her Master of Fine Arts in Studio Arts from the School of Visual Arts in New York City. She currently lives in New York City where she works as a freelance educator in the arts.

First edition for the United States and Canada published by
Barron's Educational Series, Inc., 2007.

Produced by Salamander Books,
an imprint of Anova Books Company Ltd.,
10 Southcombe Street, London W14 0RA, U.K.

All inquiries should be addressed to:
Barron's Educational Series,
250 Wireless Boulevard,
Hauppauge, New York 11788
www.barronsedu.com

ISBN-13: 978-0-7641-6089-9
ISBN-10: 0-7641-6089-3

Library of Congress Catalog Card No. 2007938866

Printed in China

9 8 7 6 5 4 3 2 1

Introduction

When seeing American Sign Language (ASL) for the first time, people often describe it as "beautiful" and "fascinating." Its endless variety of movement, sometimes slow and graceful and other times sharp and staccato, combine with playfulness and changes in facial expression to create an eloquent visual world rich in subtlety and precision. Since its beginnings in the early nineteenth century, with roots in French Sign Language, it has evolved into the dynamic language we know today through some odd twists of history and some extraordinary characters. This introduction will examine this history, and then discuss some of the many aspects of ASL that are different from English.

THE HISTORY OF ASL

In 1814, in Hartford, Connecticut, Thomas Hopkins Gallaudet was about to launch an unanticipated career change. Home after his graduation from the Andover Theological Seminary, and as his son Edward Miner Gallaudet wrote in a biography, "preaching occasionally, and waiting for some decided indication of Providence as to the path of duty," Gallaudet noticed that Alice Cogswell, the nine-year-old daughter of a neighbor, was not talking with the other children. When he learned she was deaf, he started teaching her words by writing them in the dirt and pointing to the objects they represented. "Hat" was easy enough, as were people's names, but going beyond these simple concepts was far more difficult.

Gallaudet was already an accomplished man at the age of 28. He'd entered Yale University at the age of 15 and graduated in three years. He studied law independently and did his apprenticeship, then returned to Yale to earn his Masters degree. He became a traveling salesman in Kentucky and Ohio, and was profoundly affected by the poverty suffered by rural children. This, combined with his family's strong Protestant background, led him to theology. He decided to become a traveling preacher.

As he worked with Alice, though, his priorities began to shift. Although he had considerable success with her he also became more and more aware of what he did not know. How can teaching happen without language? How can English be taught to someone who cannot hear it?

"Hearing" people study English through books, yes, but only after they spend the first years of their lives listening to it and then speaking it. And, in an echo of the religious motivation that Gallaudet would soon discover in Europe, how can those without language become true Christians?

Alice's father, Mason Fitch Cogswell, was a prominent and well-connected physician in the Hartford area. He'd long been searching for a way to educate his daughter, and knew that methods for teaching deaf children had been developed and were in use in England and France; England employed "articulation," using spoken English and lip-reading (or "speechreading") to teach deaf students, while France used sign language. He had a book of the French manual alphabet. He gathered some friends and got commitments—in one day—for enough money to send someone to Europe to learn their methods, with the goal of returning to Hartford and establishing a school for deaf children. Gallaudet was the obvious choice. After considerable hesitation, considering himself unqualified for the job, he agreed.

In London and Edinburgh he found little help and cooperation from those he anticipated would be keen to share their teaching methods. However, while in London, he met the Abbé Roch Sicard, a teacher at the school for the deaf in Paris.

The French school's approach to communication and teaching was completely different from the English articulation method. The English school emphasized making spoken language visible through speechreading and writing, and required the deaf students to express themselves with their own voices. No signs, or "manual communication" were used or permitted. Their aim was to minimize the effect of deafness by giving the students as much of the hearing world's communication as possible.

Sicard's approach was based on the recognition that people unable to hear language can best communicate with a truly visual language. In other words, if the ears aren't available, instruction must make maximum use of the eyes. But there are many facets to this simple principle. While it's true that speechreading makes use of the eyes for receiving information, it's merely a secondary form of the spoken language. The primary form of English, of course, is speech; reading and speechreading are secondary modes of receiving spoken language. Hearing people are able to learn reading and writing as well as they do, usually starting at the age of five, largely because they first spend those preceding years listening to the language and essentially mastering its primary form. What they see on the page, whether it's just a "t" or a full word, is a representation of sound to which they have attached meaning through countless repetitions and variations. There is always more vocabulary to learn, and idioms and grammatical nuances, but this is overlay; they are quite competent users of the language when they start to learn reading and writing.

It is for this reason that mastering reading and writing is an extraordinarily difficult challenge for those who lose their hearing before acquiring language. When all those words and meanings have to be learned first through the written form of the language, or, far less precisely, through speechreading (under the best circumstances, 40 percent of the English language is visible through speechreading), the process of learning the language becomes much more complicated. Speechreading and writing are not visual languages—they are visual codes for spoken languages. True sign languages come into being just as spoken languages do, through natural evolution driven by the need to communicate.

When Gallaudet arrived in France his first job was to begin learning French Sign Language (FSL). His tutor was Laurent Clerc, one of the deaf men he'd met in London, who had graduated from the school and was now its senior teacher. Various members of the faculty also taught Gallaudet their teaching methods, but it was Clerc, a man of impressive accomplishments, who was by far the biggest influence, and a deep friendship grew between them. After a few months, Gallaudet felt it was time to return to Hartford but did not feel that he'd learned enough to start a school on his own. In discussing his dilemma with Clerc, the Frenchman unexpectedly offered to accompany him back to America and help him set up the school

Gallaudet and Clerc reached Hartford on June 22nd, 1816. His sponsors had not been idle during his absence. They had secured more funding, from both private sources and the Connecticut state legislature, and on April 15, 1817, the "Connecticut Asylum for the Education and Instruction of Deaf and Dumb Persons," opened its doors with, of course, Alice Cogswell as the first of the initial group of seven students. (The phrases "Deaf and Dumb" and "Deaf-Mute," relics of another era, are today considered offensive and their use has all but disappeared.) In less than two years, as the student body grew and students from other states attended, the name

was changed to "The American Asylum at Hartford, for the Education and Instruction of the Deaf and Dumb," and finally to the American School for the Deaf, as it is known today.

As Gallaudet and Clerc, along with the faculty they recruited, began to teach their students, a language evolution took place. Students, of course, did not present themselves as linguistic *tabulae rasae*. They did not all arrive profoundly deaf; some had various degrees of "residual hearing" that could be used for learning some spoken language. Some of those who were profoundly deaf had become so not at birth but in later years—scarlet fever was a leading cause—and those students might have had several years of learning and using English before their hearing loss occurred. More significantly for the growth of ASL, many students arrived with home signs.

In the early decades of the nineteenth century, with most travel and communication in New England limited to foot and horse power, there was no way for deaf people, scattered as they were, to discover each other and congregate—meaning that there was no standardization in the signing they brought to the school. There was no language community, and no communication system can evolve into a language without a community of a certain size, a critical mass. The school provided that. Gallaudet and Clerc taught signing to the teachers, the teachers taught the students, and, most importantly and dynamically of all, the students adapted it to their own purposes. It is axiomatic of any natural language that its users will find a way to express whatever needs expressing; the teachers used signing to discuss history, math, religion, and woodworking, but the students also used this wonderful visual language—with no struggling to read lips and printed words, a language to which they could apply their own creativity—to discuss all those serious and frivolous things that children and adolescents everywhere do, and to play, poke fun at their teachers and dorm supervisors, and laugh together.

This was not the only use of signing in the New World at that time. The plains Indians used signs for communication between tribes when there was no common spoken language, although this appears to have been more a collection of vocabulary than an actual language. (One sign for "to die," simple and clear, was the index finger held up vertically in front of the signer, then gradually falling forward to the horizontal.) And on the island of Martha's Vineyard, off the coast of Massachusetts, hereditary deafness grew in the limited gene pool to the point where such a large percentage of the population was deaf—twice the national average in all, but up to 50 percent in some places—that their own variety of signing was in effect a second language for the island. There were so many deaf people, mixing and marrying freely amongst both themselves and the hearing population, that signing was often used as a matter of course in public areas.

But these other varieties of signing seem to have had limited impact on the deaf community of New England in the 1800s, and so ASL today is a combination of French Sign Language and the home signs that arrived with the students, all mixed together in a joyous cauldron fueled by human imagination and creativity.

Inventor Alexander Graham Bell possessed a powerful intellect of extraordinary depth and breadth, and his interests ranged from the medical to the agricultural to the mechanical. His strongest passion in life, however, was not the kind of pursuit that led to his invention of the telephone. The son and grandson of "elocutionists"—public speakers and speech therapists— his great interest was teaching speech to deaf people. Even his signature invention was the result of an agreement with his bride's father, Gardiner Hubbard. A lawyer and entrepreneur, Hubbard agreed to provide financial support to the new family, enabling Bell to pursue speech teaching. In return, Bell was required to devote a specified number of hours each day to his work on the telephone, which Hubbard saw as a great investment opportunity.

Mabel Hubbard, Bell's wife, was his first student. She was deaf but never learned sign language. This fitted into Bell's image of a successful deaf person; his mother was hard of hearing, and although she had trouble speechreading, she was able to engage in conversations and played the piano.

In Europe, the education of deaf people was still split into two camps: the "oralists," who felt that all deaf people could be taught to speak and should therefore be educated through those means exclusively, and the "manualists," who believed that a natural visual language was best for communicating with and teaching deaf students. When the controversy spilled across the Atlantic, the oralists found a ready and energetic champion in Alexander Bell.

The basis of the disagreement went far beyond teaching methods. At its core were opposing views on what the very purpose of deaf education should be. For Bell and the oralists, it was solely to enable them to integrate into the larger hearing world; they viewed deafness as something of a calamity (although this was merely a stronger form of a common attitude—even Clerc referred to deaf people as "poor unfortunates"), and its only proper mitigation was to make them, in

effect, less deaf. For the manualists the goal was broader: the development of deaf people to their maximum potential. While Thomas Gallaudet and his son Edward Miner Gallaudet, who carried forward his father's work, tried to turn their students into educated, happy and well-adjusted deaf adults, Bell wanted them to become as much like hearing people as possible.

Astonishingly, the reason Bell was so unalterably opposed to the use of signing in education was also a major reason Edward Gallaudet supported it: it is so very effective. Gallaudet appreciated how well sign language can impart information to those who can't hear, and how natural and comfortable manual communication can be. Bell knew this also, but felt that deaf students who knew sign language would use it whenever possible, to the detriment of learning speech skills.

At two European conferences of the International Congress of Educators of the Deaf, in 1880 and 1900, the oralists swept aside the manualists with the cry, "*Vive la parole*! Long live speech!" These were decisions made by hearing people; at the second conference, when deaf participants arrived to support the manualist cause, they were denied participation. One member justified the exclusion, and illuminated the attitude of the conference, this way: "Since when does the physician consult with the patient on the nature of the cure?"

What followed was something of a dark age for sign language in America. In the oralist tide that swept the country, most deaf teachers were fired, regardless of talent, dedication and experience. No signing was permitted in the classroom, and it was often forbidden on the playground as well. Hands were slapped and punishments given for those caught communicating with their hands. The goal was to eradicate signing in the schools by forbidding its use, but the horse was already well out of the barn. Languages aren't eliminated by rules and policies. Signing continued to thrive in dorm rooms and on playgrounds when no one was looking simply because it was the best way to communicate.

In 1960, a hearing English teacher named William Stokoe was on the faculty of Gallaudet College. Sign language was the *lingua franca* of the college, of course, but nationally it held a lowly status, generally considered something less than a language, mere broken English and gestures. Stokoe saw something else—he noticed that every time a signer asked a yes/no question, the signers' eyebrows went up at the end of the sentence. He studied other signers, and noticed that they all did this. He quickly broadened his research and had soon identified many other behaviors among signers that were used consistently and uniformly. He had discovered that ASL was governed by grammatical rules—that ASL was a true language. In 1965 he published *A Dictionary Of American Sign Language On Linguistic Principles.*

This was the nudge that turned the battleship. With signing recognized as a language, schools for the deaf began to rethink their insistence on oralism. Many years had passed since the height of Bell's influence, and the civil rights movement stimulated a greater openness to Gallaudet's perspective on human potential as it related to deaf students. Schools for the deaf began to adopt signing, but not yet ASL. Instead, they generally used manual codes for English—while they accepted that speech was less important than had been believed in the past, they recognized the value of reading and writing skills, and thought signing which presented English visually would be most effective. A Tower of Babel emerged as invented systems sprouted during the 1970s: Seeing Exact English, Seeing Essential English, Linguistics of Visual English (LOVE), etc. Some were logical and attempted to add common sense visual markers to ASL vocabulary, and some were nightmares of language butchery that served only to confuse. By the 1990s these artificial systems were waning in schools for the deaf (and the use of ASL growing), although they held on longer in "mainstream" programs where deaf students are taught in their local public schools with interpreters alongside their hearing peers. The latest strong signing movement in deaf education is the "bi-lingual/bi-cultural" approach—giving deaf students a strong foundation in their natural visual language, ASL, and the culture of the American deaf community, while also teaching them English as a second language.

Throughout all these changes, and the overlays of hearing paternalism, however well-meaning, ASL has maintained its position as the natural language among the American deaf population.

Today there is greater use and acceptance of ASL than ever before. It is the fourth most used language in America. The National Association of the Deaf, formed in 1880 to counteract the oralist movement, has some 20,000 members; their biennial conferences draw about 2,000 participants from all over the country for workshops, arts and celebrations (they tend to take over the conference hotels, turning the tables on the hearing businessman who finds himself the only person in the elevator that doesn't know what everyone's laughing about). Thousands of college and university ASL classes are offered every semester, often with long waiting lists. Many colleges and high schools around the country accept ASL for fulfilment of foreign language requirements.

Why? ASL is a beautiful and playful language, and it's fun. It's extremely plastic; signs can be changed, or inflected, in large and small ways to convey a huge range of meanings. Its graceful movements provide endless possibilities for humor. Stories in ASL are visual journeys; characters disappear and reappear with a glance, plot lines diverge and twist, and worlds are created in space, all guided by the signer's personality and creativity.

Gallaudet College is now Gallaudet University and is the only liberal arts college for deaf students in the world. In 1968 congress created the National Technical Institute for the Deaf, nested in a hearing university as one of the colleges of the Rochester Institute of Technology; both Gallaudet University and NTID have about 1,200 students, most from the 50 states but many from around the world.

LINGUISTICS OF AMERICAN SIGN LANGUAGE

The most obvious difference between ASL and English is, of course, that it's a visual language. But let's examine this a little more deeply. A spoken language like English enters the brain for processing through the ear. This is an entirely passive process. Ears never become fatigued with this process because no muscles are involved—it's not work. Brains may become tired from trying to understand what's being heard, but not the ear.

Not so the eye, which works like a muscle to focus on images. Eyes do become tired. Partly because of this, ASL has evolved in a way that is more spatial than linear. Instead of spoken words following each other one by one, ASL uses the "signing space" in front of the signer's body to convey a lot of information simultaneously. For example, the English phrase "that boy over there," requiring the four words spoken consecutively, can be rendered in ASL in an instant, with one hand signing BOY and the other pointing to over there. The sign HAPPY requires not just a movement of the hands, but a matching facial expression; to express "very happy," no additional sign is needed. Instead, the movement of the hands is changed (inflected), and the facial expression increased accordingly, to modify the meaning.

THE NATURE OF SIGNS

There are certain conventions in the production of signs, and learning them helps in understanding how the language works. Sometimes called the "parameters" of signs, these are handshape, location, movement, and palm orientation. (As we'll see below, facial expression and other non-manual behaviors are very important when vocabulary is used in sentences, but these four describe the basics of how vocabulary is produced.) These parameters are pretty self-explanatory—handshape is the shape made with the fingers and palm, location is where the sign is made (near the forehead, at the chest, etc.), movement is where the hands start and finish during the sign (right to left, up to down, across the chin, etc.), and palm orientation refers to which direction the palms are facing during the sign (left, right, in, down, etc.).

It's good to get a grasp of these parameters, as a subtle change in just one of them can make quite a difference. The signs COFFEE and MAKE have exactly the same handshape, location and palm orientation, and are differentiated only by a subtle difference in movement. FATHER and MOTHER are identical in movement, handshape and orientation, and only the location is different.

ASL has both iconic and arbitrary signs. Iconic signs look like what they mean, and there are many of them; it's one of the reasons ASL is so much fun to learn and use. The sign for TREE is the right forearm raised vertically from the elbow, which is based on the back of the flat left hand, palm down. The right hand's five fingers are splayed out and wiggling. In this we can easily see a trunk with branches and leaves at the top. HOUSE is signed with two flat hands whose fingertips meet pointing up at an angle, showing the peak of a roof; the two hands then move out and down, indicating the walls. GO is two index fingers moving towards a direction, and COME is two index fingers moving toward the signer. ACCEPT is two open hands closing to "O" handshapes at the chest. The sign SPIDER looks like … well, like a spider. (A spoken language like English has no visual iconicity, of course, but has something similar in onomatopoeia, where a word sounds like what it means—click, clink, boom, swish, buzz.)

Another kind of iconicity can be seen, we believe, in some signs that have come to us from FSL. The sign for female is an "A" handshape with the thumb moving down the side of the jaw a couple of times, and this is said to represent the strap of a French woman's bonnet; likewise, the sign for male, an "O" handshape opening and closing twice above the signer's forehead, would reflect the brim of a Frenchman's hat. Many signs having to do with gender incorporate these locations: SON, SISTER, BROTHER, NIECE, NEPHEW, etc. Other signs that seem to have come from FSL are examples of initialization—using the first letter of a spoken language's word, together with movement, to create a sign for that meaning. SEE is a "V" handshape, palm toward the signer, moving out from the eye, and *voir* is the French word for see. LOOK FOR is a

"C" handshape circling in front of the face, likely from the French word *chercher*. These signs probably go back to FSL as it evolved among the students and teachers at the French school and was brought to America by Thomas Gallaudet and Laurent Clerc.

Arbitrary signs have no apparent visual relation to their meaning. ALCOHOL is the right fist bouncing on the left; both hands have the index and little fingers extended. APPLE is an "X" handshape twisting at the cheek. INSECT is a "3" handshape with the thumb touching the nose and the other two fingers crooking in a couple of times, and SOON is the "F" handshape with the thumb and forefinger together bouncing on the chin; obviously, these signs' meaning cannot be guessed from what they look like.

ASL has its own ways of handling time and verb tenses. In English, verbs must agree with the time frame: "I worked yesterday until 3:00, then I went home." In ASL, once the time has been established in a conversation or story, that is the assumed tense until someone changes it. In an ASL translation of the example above, there would be no indication in the production of the sign for work that it's past tense; the sign yesterday takes care of it. When no time indication is signed, it usually means the present tense is being used.

Signs also make use of the "time line," running from behind the signer's right shoulder, over it and forward (past to future), to add a wide variety of options for using time and space. A flat straight handshape moving forward along this line (see the sign WILL) means in the general future; farther forward means farther into the future. A flat handshape bending and waving back over the shoulder means the past, and a longer movement means farther back in time. Facial expression is necessary also; the sign inflection meaning "very recently" is accompanied by squinting eyes, pursed lips and the right shoulder and chin moving closer together. "Far in the past" involves puffed cheeks, wide eyes and a slight lean back. "Once upon a time" has two flat hands moving back over the right shoulder in complementary circles; the larger the circles, the more distant the time.

Signs can take advantage of the time line in other ways. The sign FAIL, repeated a few times, each a bit forward from the last, means "will fail repeatedly into the future." Sometimes the hands aren't even needed to change the time; a simple quick lifting of the right shoulder towards the chin while telling a story (with the appropriate facial expression, of course) brings the time closer to the present from the past, and these indications are always relative to the context of the story. When talking about something that happened a few decades ago, a slight shoulder lift could mean "but in recent years" and a more pronounced lift could mean "in recent months." If the context is a couple of weeks ago, a shoulder lift could mean "the other day."

Because signed languages do not have written forms, and video technology has only recently made sign language recordings possible, we have little direct evidence of the changes that ASL has undergone as it evolved on this side of the Atlantic. But some early writings and a bit of fascinating film footage from 1914, produced by the National Association of the Deaf, give us some glimpses. HELP was once signed with the right palm supporting the bent left elbow and moving it forward; today, probably for reasons of economy, the right palm is under the left fist in an "A" handshape. Other changes have taken place with the signs for LOVE and HAVE.

USE OF SPACE AND PRONOUNS

When referring to nouns in an English conversation, whether people, places, objects or even concepts, we use their labels and names: Emily; Rome; the car. For a shortcut, we use pronouns: she, it, us, and so on. ASL pronouns use space. For example, if the signer is talking about Emily, but she's not present, he identifies her and points in the general direction of where she is or where the signer places her for the purposes of the story. After that, the signer need only to point there again to refer to her (this is called indexing). This way of handling pronouns often gives them greater precision and economy than English pronouns. ASL can use indexing for two or three people, and because they are placed in exact locations, who's being referred to is always clear. In a story about a fishing trip, for instance, once the characters have been identified ASL can talk about their interactions using only pronouns—pointing to the people you're talking about. If you tried this in English, it would wind up like this: "When my father and my brothers Al and Fred got to the lake, he turned to him and said…" We're already lost!

VERB DIRECTIONALITY AND ADVERBS

Space can be even more dynamically used in a signed conversation or story with verb directionality. To show interactions among people and things, English uses word order and prepositions: "My mother helped me;" "I borrowed money from the bank." ASL uses space and verb directionality to express the same meanings, reducing the number of signs needed. In context, because the locations of my mother and me are

established, the signer need only inflect the basic sign HELP, moving it in a line from Mom to herself. By varying her effect and the sign's movement, she can also convey her mother's attitude about the whole thing and how much or often she does it; whether she's helping willingly or reluctantly, whether it's hard or easy, and whether she helps once, repeatedly, or over a long period of time. With these inflections, ASL needs just one sign to say: "My mother reluctantly helped me over and over."

CLASSIFIERS

Classifiers are handshapes that specify what an object is doing or its shape, and sometimes both. They have meaning only when referring to an established noun, whether by label or context. A "3" handshape, positioned horizontally with the palm in, can represent a car, a hay wagon, an ocean liner or a rowboat—any land or water vehicle—but it must be identified first. Movements of the hand can say that the vehicle is going forward, backward, fast, slow, sinking, etc. Other handshapes are used to show thinness, roundness, a spill, a mound, etc. A very thin, round object like a dowel or pipe is described with two "F" handshapes moving away from each other, accompanied by pursed lips, narrowed eyes and hunched shoulders. A very thick round pipe is shown by two "C" handshapes moving away from each other with wide eyes and puffed cheeks. Once again, the facial expression and other aspects of inflection are critical; describing a pipe incorrectly with "F" handshapes and puffed cheeks would be equivalent to the nonsensical "the thick thin pipe."

FACIAL EXPRESSION AND BUILDING SENTENCES

While ASL is correctly described as an expressive language due to the emotions visible on the signer's face, as we've seen already, facial expressions have other important responsibilities. English changes the word order and adds helping verbs to change a statement to a question ("He went downtown" versus "Did he go downtown?"), but in ASL, the difference between the two sentences is that the question is signed with raised eyebrows, sometimes with a slight forward tilt of the head, and briefly holding the last sign. "Wh-" questions, those asking what, who, when, why, how many, etc., are usually signed with the wh- sign at the end, and require an eyebrows-down expression, similar to a frown, during the part of the sentence containing the wh- sign.

SENTENCE STRUCTURE AND WORD ORDER

ASL's word order, or syntax, can be similar to English when signing short, simple sentences (subject-verb-object), but longer sentences require the use of topic/comment structure. While it's fine to sign, "I like ice cream" in the same word order as the English, the sentence "I like that new restaurant over by the baseball statue" would start with its topic, restaurant, followed by signs and the use of space to specify it as the new one over by the baseball statue (these parts signed with an eyebrows-up facial expression), and ending with the point of the whole sentence, or the comment: that the signer likes it (eyebrows back down and a slight nod). There is always more than one way to translate something, but a description in English of how to sign this sentence could look like this: "[raised eyebrows] RESTAURANT NEW [point in the direction of the restaurant; point higher for farther away, lower for closer] BASEBALL STATUE NEAR, LIKE [eyebrows down with the verb and a slight head nod. The sign for I in this case is optional, as long as it's clear that the speaker is talking about her own opinion].

Complicated? Well, certainly no more than the nuances and idiosyncrasies of English (where the meanings of "slow up" and "slow down" are not opposite but identical, "through" rhymes with "rue" but not "tough," and "putting the dog on the leash" is the same as "putting the leash on the dog"). These basic principles of structure and inflection pervade ASL, and once they're learned and internalized everything starts to fall into place. Students often describe a series of plateaus when developing their skills; what's mysterious today starts to make sense tomorrow (well, maybe next week), and, as with any new language, classes and media and studying are best combined with conversing with native users of the language.

When these and other aspects of ASL signs and sentences are put together, the result is a playful, creative, and beautiful language of great precision and eloquence. As you study this book and watch skilled signers display their craft, you'll gain a fuller appreciation of the whole range of communication available to us. Have fun!

Geoffrey S. Poor, October 2007

Using The Dictionary

RIGHT AND LEFT HANDEDNESS

Some signs, such as MEETING, have both hands making the same movement with the same handshape, and some use only one hand, such as WOMAN. Many however, have the two hands using different handshapes and, to a much lesser extent, different movements. For these signs, the dominant hand (the right for right-handed people and the left for left-handed people) usually makes the movement you notice, and the other usually remains still, as in MOVIE, or makes only a very small and barely perceptible complementary movement. A good example of this is COFFEE; the hand on the bottom actually does make a tiny movement, reflecting what the top hand does, but it's not generally noticed. (Of course, this changes if the signer has a cup of coffee or a stack of books in one hand.)

In this book, our ASL model Christine Kim is right-handed and signs accordingly. Readers who are left-handed will want to reverse the hands, so that it's their left hand that makes the greater movement. (An exception is the sign for motorcycle; one look and you'll see why.)

FACIAL EXPRESSION AND BODY MOVEMENTS

As discussed above, facial expression is critical in ASL. When using this book, keep an eye on Christine's excellent facial expressions and her skillful use of other subtle bits of affect. This affect is often not necessary with nouns like HOUSE, but other signs will be misunderstood without it. TIRED will send a very mixed and confusing message if the signer doesn't look tired, and WHO will not be perceived as a question if the signer doesn't furrow the eyebrows. CROWDED won't really mean crowded if the face is impassive and the shoulders are not drawn in.

NOTE ON SYNONYMS

Many signs can be translated by more than one English word, even when those English words do not mean exactly the same thing. The sign for "president," for example, can also mean "superintendent." The synonyms listed next to the photographs in this dictionary are other words that the signs can mean. The index at the back lists the English words for signs used in this dictionary.

The Alphabet

A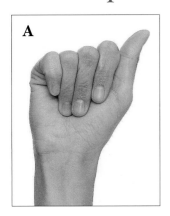

B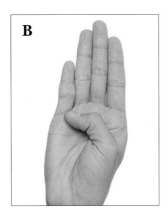

C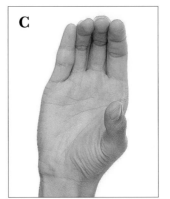

D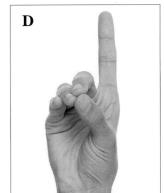

E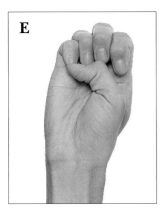

F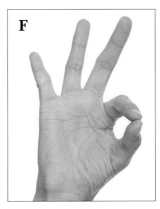

G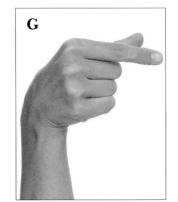

H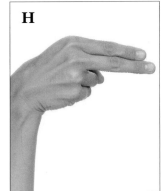

I

J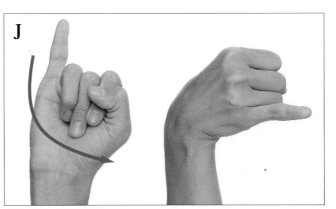

K

L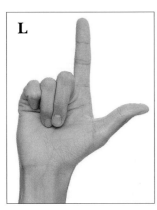

M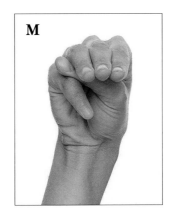

N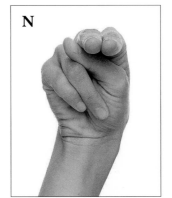

O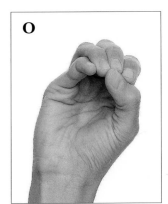

The Alphabet

P

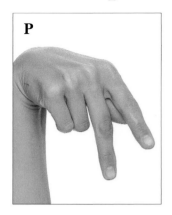

Q

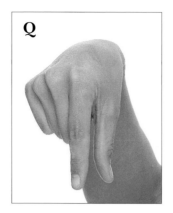

R

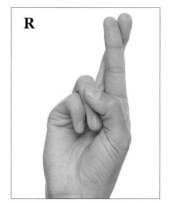

S

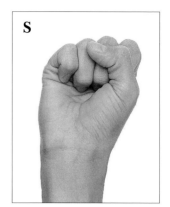

T

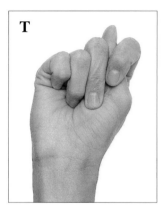

U

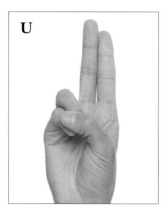

V

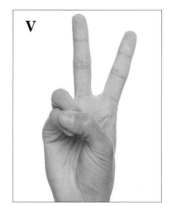

W

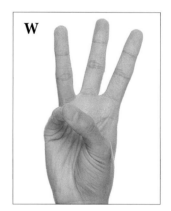

X

Y

Z-Make a "Z" in the air

ABANDON
Palms sweep up and face out

Synonyms—Surrender, give up

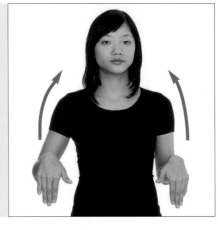

ABOUT (CONCERNING)
Index finger circles out, down and around closed left hand

Synonym—Concerning

ABOVE
Right hand arcs slightly to the right and up from left

ACCEPT
Open out hands, move inward and close against chest

ACT
Alternately brush thumbs against chest with small inward circles

Synonyms—Play, theater, show, drama, perform

ADD TO
Move open right hand up and in, closing to meet left hand, in a grab motion

ADDRESS
Move both hands, with thumbs upward, in two circular motions

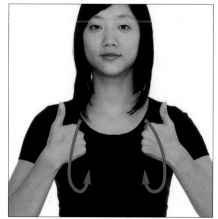

ADVERTISE
Right fist moves forward and opens from in front of left fist. Repeat motion

ADVISE
Closed handshape on back of left hand opens and moves forward

Synonym—To counsel

AFRAID
Move both hands toward center of chest. Repeat motion

Synonyms—Scared, fearful

AFRICA
Close hand in front of chest; open hand, and bring hand down, closing fingers

AFTER

Slide upright hand over back of left hand

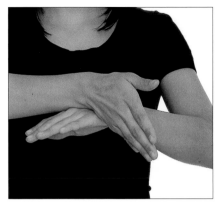

AFTERNOON

Elbow of right forearm rests on back of left hand; right hand waves down. Repeat motion

AGAIN

Bent fingers arc onto palm of other hand

Synonym—Repeat

AGAINST

Straight fingers of right hand move in straight line into palm of left hand

Synonym—Oppose

AGREE
Right index finger touches side of head, then moves down to rest parallel to left index finger

AHEAD
With thumbs stretched upward, right hand arcs around, forward and stops in front of left hand

AIR CONDITIONER
Move hand from "A" handshape to "C" handshape

AIRPLANE

Stretch out forefinger and
little finger and move hand
through air, right to left.
Repeat motion

ALARM

Forefinger taps twice
against left palm

ALCOHOL

Stretch out forefinger and little
finger and bring hand down
onto identical left handshape.
Repeat motion

Synonym—Liquor

ALL

Right hand sweeps in front,
around and behind left hand, and
turns to rest in left palm

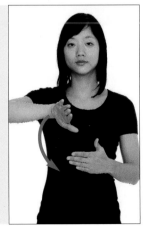  

ALL OVER

Open hand with five fingers spread; sweep in wide counterclockwise arc

Synonym—Everywhere

ALL RIGHT

Flat upright hand slides up and forward across left palm, before being lifted upward. Repeat motion

Synonyms—Okay, fine

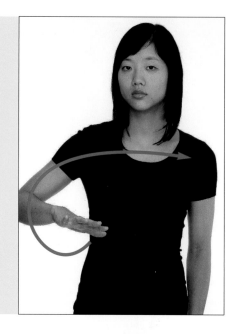

ALLERGY

Touch tip of nose with index finger, bring both index fingers together and then draw them apart

ALLIGATOR

Place palms together, fingers out-stretched; lift top hand vertically and bring down twice

Synonym—Crocodile

ALLOW

Parallel hands sweep up and forward

Synonym—Permit

ALMOST

Fingers of bent right hand move up back of bent left-hand fingers

Synonym—Nearly

ALONE

Forearm with extended index finger describes two small, counterclockwise circles from elbow

Synonym—Single

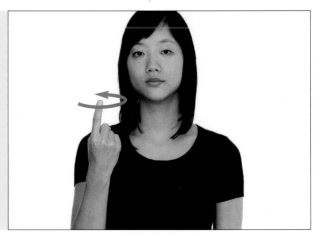

ALTERNATE
"L" handshape sweeps to left side and back

ALWAYS
Forearm with extended index finger describes two large, counterclockwise circles from elbow

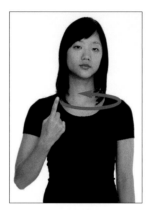

AMAZED
Two fists open quickly into claw shapes and close again

Synonym—Surprised

AMBULANCE
Outstretched fingers rotate back and forth at either side of head

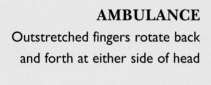

AMERICA

Interlock fingers in front of body with thumbs outstretched; rotate arms counterclockwise

ANALYZE

"V" handshapes move down while crooking fingers twice

AND

Open hand closes as it moves right across body

ANGRY

Claw hand in front of body arcs up and out past face

Synonym—Mad (with rage)

ANNOUNCE

Touch index fingers to chin and sweep them down and away from each other

 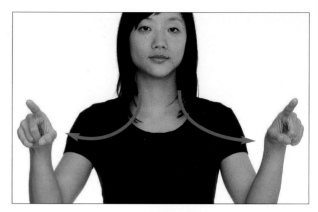

ANSWER

Index fingers, right at chin, left in front, move down and forward

Synonyms—Respond, reply

ANXIOUS

Bend middle fingers and alternately touch chest, then swing out and back in small arcs

Synonyms—Nervous, concerned, worried

ANY

Clench fist with thumb stretched out and rotate hand in front of body

ANYONE

Clench fist with thumb outstretched, turn hand down then up, hide thumb and point index finger upward

ANYWAY

With fingers together, thumbs outstretched, alternately bring hands toward and away from body, fingertips touching as they pass

APPEAR (SHOW UP)

Index finger rises up between index and middle fingers of left hand

APPLAUD

Clap hands together. Repeat motion

Synonym—Compliment

APPLE

Crook index finger and rotate against cheek. Repeat motion

APPLY

With thumb and index finger, pull shirt slightly out and back twice

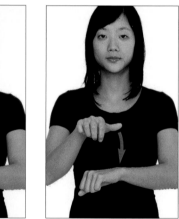

APPOINTMENT

Rotate open hand; close to "A" handshape and place on back of other hand

Synonym—Reservation

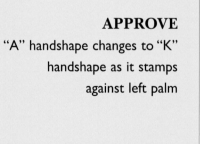

APPROVE

"A" handshape changes to "K" handshape as it stamps against left palm

APPROXIMATELY
Open hand, palm out,
and rotate slowly
counterclockwise

Synonym—About (roughly)

AREA
Open hand, palm down,
describes a couple of
counterclockwise circles

ARREST
Open hands then close them
together at wrists while
fists close

ARRIVE
Bring down back of fingers on
palm of other hand

ART
Little finger moves down palm twice

ARTICLE
Thumb and bent index finger move down palm twice

ARTIFICIAL
Index finger moves across and down past nose

ASHAMED
Wipe back of fingers against cheek and bring hand forward and down

ASK
Straight index finger bends and moves out and down

Synonyms—Inquire, question

ASSIGN
Fork index and middle finger over index finger of other hand

ASSISTANT
Clench fists and outstretch thumbs; tap thumb against base of left fist twice

ASSOCIATE WITH
Open hands and rotate fingertips around each other

Synonym—Mingle

ATTEND

Outstretch index fingers and point hands down and forward. Repeat motion

ATTITUDE

The "A" handshape circles and the back of the thumb lands at the opposite shoulder

ATTRACTED TO

Open hand in front of face moves down and forward to clenched fist

Synonym—Fascinated

AUDIENCE

Outstretch hands close together in front of body, then bring back toward shoulders as fingers bend

AUNT

Place "A" handshape at side of face and rock slightly

AVERAGE

Tap vertical hand twice against horizontal left hand so that little finger hits at middle

Synonym—Medium

AVOID

With thumbs up, move back hand away from front left hand

AWKWARD

Stretch out thumb, index, and middle fingers then alternately move each hand up and down in front of body

Synonym—Clumsy

From Baby to Buy

BABY
Mime rocking a baby

BAD
Place fingertips to lips then move hand down with palm facing downward

BAKE
Mime placing object in oven; lower hand, palm-up, slides forward under left hand

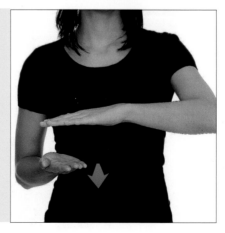 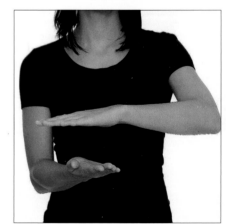

BALANCE
Place right hand at head level, left at shoulder, fingers and palms at right angles; alternately move hands up and down

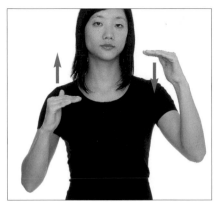

BANANA
Mime peeling banana skin, using index finger as banana

BARELY
Draw index finger and thumb together, outward from right side of upper forehead

BASEBALL
Imitate holding baseball bat, swing hands backward and forward

BASEMENT

Circle right fist with thumb extended under left palm twice

Synonym—Cellar

BASIC

Circle right hand under left palm twice

BASKETBALL

Mime swivelling basketball between thumb, index, and middle fingers. Repeat motion

BEAR (ANIMAL)

Cross arms and scratch shoulders with claw hands in small circles

BECAUSE

Touch forehead with index finger, then move hand away from head, thumb in air

Synonym—Since

BECOME

Cross palms together in front of body; reverse position of hands in a sweep across chest, keeping palms together

BED

Lean head to side and and tap twice with palm of hand

BEER

Brush side of cheek twice with fingers, palm facing out

BEFORE

Right hand moves back toward shoulder from behind left hand

Synonyms—Former, past

BEG

Place back of hand on top of left palm, then make grasping motions with upper hand

Synonym—Plead

BELIEVE
Touch head with index finger and lower hand to clasp left palm

BELL
Closed right hand taps twice against upright palm of left hand like a bell clapper

BELOW
With fingers at right angles to palms, meet fingertips in front of body and move right hand down

Synonym—Less than

 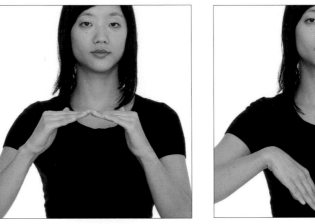

BENEFIT
Thumb and index finger strike chest gently while hand moves downward from wrist. Repeat motion

BEST

Raise fingers toward mouth and move hand up and out to side of head, thumb extended

BET

Place hands, palms facing, in front of body and lower, palms down, as though covering cards

BETTER

Raise fingers toward mouth and move hand out to side of head, thumb extended

BETWEEN

Slide upright hand back and forth twice between thumb and index finger of left hand

BICYCLE

Clench fists and imitate forward peddling motion

BIG

Thumb and bent index finger handshapes approach each other and draw apart

Synonym—Large

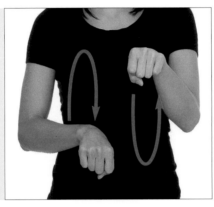

BIOLOGY

"B" handshapes describe alternating circles on a vertical plane

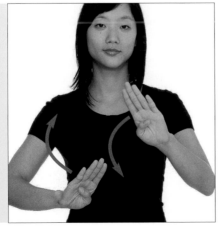

BIRTHDAY
Touch bent middle finger to chin and then to center of chest

BLACK
Draw side of index finger across forehead left to right

BLIND
Move bent index and middle fingers in toward eyes

BLOUSE
Place open hands in front of shoulders; bring both hands down in an arc to lower torso

B

BLOW UP (TEMPER)

Abruptly bring up and slam down
palm of open hand onto
left clenched fist

Synonym—Rage

BLUE

"B" handshape rotates outward
at wrist. Repeat motion

BOAST

Alternately bring thumbs in to
touch waist and out again

Synonym—Brag

BOAT

Cup hands; move down
and forward and back up again,
then end with hands down
and forward

Synonym—Ship

41

BODY

Place hands on chest near shoulders; bring both hands down to the waist

BOIL (WITH ANGER)

Wiggle fingertips beneath palm of left hand

BOOK

Place palms together, then imitate opening and closing book. Repeat motion

BORING

Twist index finger at side of nose

BORN

Slide lower hand forward
underneath the palm of the
upper hand

Synonym—Birth

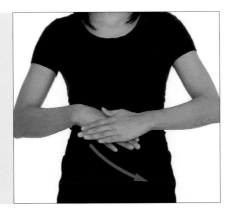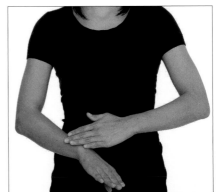

BORROW

With right "V" handshape on left,
move hands back toward body

Synonym—Lend

BOSS

Make hand claw shaped and tap
shoulder with fingertips twice

Synonym—Captain

BOTH

Make fork shape with middle and
index finger and draw through
left hand, from top to bottom,
while closing fingers

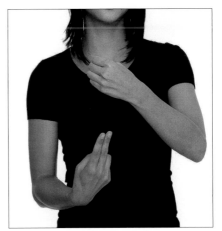

BOTHER

Using chopping motion, strike other hand between thumb and index finger twice

BOWLING

Imitate grasping ball in hand; sway arm back and forth twice

BOY

Close hand twice at forehead

Synonym—Male

BRACELET

Clasp other wrist with thumb and index finger and bounce once

BRAVE

Place claw-shaped fingers on front of shoulders, then bring hands out to form fists

Synonyms—Confident, healthy

BREAD

Bent hand moves along back of other hand with short downward movements

BREAK (DAMAGE)

Joined fists break down and away

BREAKFAST

Bring fingertips to lips, then open out arm in front of body and touch inside of right elbow with left hand

BREATHE
Place right hand on chest and left on abdomen; lift hands away from body and back in again

BRIDGE
Touch index and middle finger to wrist and again near elbow

BRING
Mime lifting an object from one side of body in toward the body

Synonym—Carry

BROKE (NO MONEY)
Using chopping motion, tap side of neck with hand

BROTHER

Touch thumb of "L" handshape against forehead and swing down to rest on top of left hand

BROWN

Fold thumb in and stroke side of cheek with hand, palm out

BUG (INSECT)

Touch nose with thumb, with middle and index fingers outstretched; then crook middle and index fingers twice

Synonym—Insect

BUILD

Move hands up and down in front of body so that tips of fingers touch when they pass

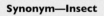

BULLETIN BOARD
Mime sticking up a poster; press thumbs at top and bottom

BURP
Place fist next to chest; slide hand up and point index finger at throat

BURY
"V" handshape moves down past left hand

BUSY
"B" handshape moves back and forth along back of left wrist. Repeat motion

B

BUT

Cross index fingers in front of chest and move outward

Synonym—However

BUTTER

Stroke index and middle finger inward twice on left palm

BUTTERFLY

Lock thumbs together and flap other fingers toward chest twice

BUY

Closed hand moves outward from left palm

CALIFORNIA

Touch index finger to ear and lower hand, little finger and thumb outstretched; shake hand forward in front of shoulder

CALL (SUMMON)

In one motion, right hand taps back of left hand and pulls back to "A" handshape

Synonym—Summon

CAMERA

Mime taking a photo, using index finger to click shutter twice

CAMP

Bring tips of little and index fingers together; move hand apart and downward twice

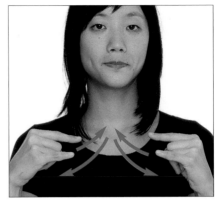

CAN (ABLE)

Fists at shoulder level, move down in front of body

CANADA

Stretch out thumb and tap on body twice between shoulder and chest

CANCEL

Draw "X" on left palm with index finger

CANDLE

Touch index finger to wrist of upright right hand and wiggle fingers of right hand

CANDY

Touch index finger to cheek and rotate finger forward and back twice

CAN'T

Index finger strikes down across left index finger

Synonym—Unable

CAPTION

"F" handshapes meet at thumb and index fingers and pull apart. Repeat motion

CAR
Grip hands and mime
steering a wheel

Synonym—Automobile

(BE) CAREFUL
"V" handshape taps twice on
left "V" handshape

Synonym—Cautious

CAREFUL
"V" handshapes circle forward
together twice, right on left

CARELESS
"V" handshapes swing down
across front of face and
back again

CAT
Bring thumb and index finger together and mime stroking a whisker twice

CATCH UP
Right fist with thumb extended moves forward to butt against left hand

CATHOLIC
Place middle and index finger together and make sign of cross in front of face

CAUSE (VERB)
With left fist behind right separate hands, stretch fingers, and move hands outward

CELEBRATE

Crook index fingers and rotate both hands at side of head

CENT

Index finger touches side of head and pulls away

CERTIFICATE

Thumbs of "C" handshapes tap together twice

CHAIR

Curved index and middle fingers move down twice onto straight index and middle fingers of left hand

CHALLENGE
Fists with thumbs extended
swing up to meet at knuckles

Synonym—Dare

CHAMPION
Bring claw hand palm down onto
tip of left index finger

CHANGE (MODIFY)
Bring "A" handshapes together,
right on left, and turn over to
reverse positions

CHARACTER (PERSONAL)

"C" handshape makes small counterclockwise circle and ends on shoulder

CHARGE (CREDIT CARD)

Slide fist along left palm, from fingertips to wrist, and back out again

Synonym—Credit card

CHASE

Stick both thumbs up and rotate back right hand in repeated circles

CHAT

Open handshapes on both hands, move up and down a few times

CHEAP
Strike left hand a downward glancing blow

CHEAT
Fork middle and index finger over fingers of other hand

CHEERFUL
Spread hands and wiggle fingers at either side of face as hands move up. Repeat motion

Synonyms—Friendly, pleasant

CHEESE
Join hands at base of palms; swivel through an arc of 45 degrees back and forth

C

CHEMISTRY

"C" handshapes move alternately in vertical in-and-out circles

CHICKEN

Thumb and index fingers form beak that closes twice

CHILDREN

Hands flat, palms down, make patting motion in center, side, and further out from body

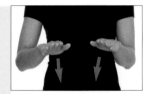
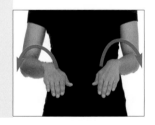 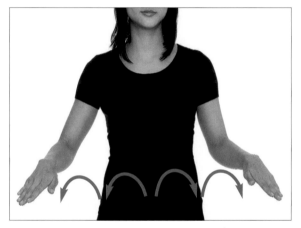

CHINA

Tip of index finger draws a right angle across body from shoulder to shoulder and down to waist

59

CHOCOLATE

Move back of thumb in a circular motion on back of other hand

CHOOSE

Using thumb and index finger, mime picking something from tip of middle finger on other hand

CIGAR

Place middle finger over index finger, place hand close to mouth, and tap wrist against chin twice

CIGARETTE

Mime holding cigarette between index and middle finger; tap side of mouth twice

CITY
Form inverted "V" by tapping fingertips together twice

Synonym—Town

CLASS
Open hands and move down and back toward each other as if cupping a ball from back to front

CLEAN (ADJECTIVE)
Wipe inside of fingers against palm of other hand, from base of palm to fingertips

Synonym—Neat (tidy)

CLEAN UP (VERB)
Slide inside of fingers twice along palm of other hand, from base of palm to beyond fingertips

CLEAR

Bring thumbs and fingertips together in front of chest; draw hands up and away, spreading fingers, palms out

Synonym—Obvious

CLOSE (VERB)

Fold thumbs in, hands at either side of shoulders; bring together in center so that palms face out

CLOSET

Cross inside of index and middle fingers; tap against each other, then reverse position, top to bottom

CLOTHES

Brush thumb tips of open hands down chest twice

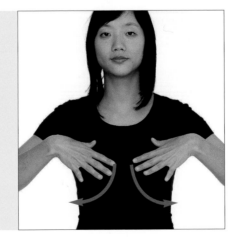

CLOUDS
Claw handshapes, right palm down and left up, rotate around each other while moving across body

 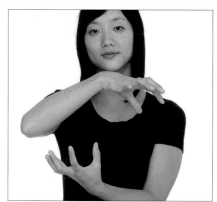

COFFEE
Right fist rotates in grinding motion on left fist

COLD (ADJECTIVE)
Hunch shoulders and make shivering motion with fists

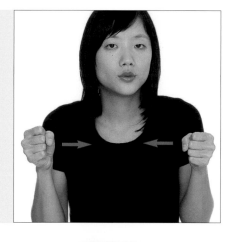 

COLD (NOUN)
Curl fingers in and pull hand down twice over nose, between index finger and outstretched thumb

COLLEGE
Slide right palm out, forward and up over left

COLOR
Wiggle fingertips against chin

COMB
Mime combing hair

COME
Point index fingers up and move hands toward self

COMFORTABLE

Rub palm of right hand across and down back of left hand; reverse hands and repeat

COMMAND

Place side of index finger on chin and move sideways in one motion and point outward in front of body

Synonym—Order

COMMUNICATE

Alternately move "C" handshapes in and away from mouth

COMMUTE

With thumb up, move hand diagonally out from shoulder and back again twice

COMPARE

Place hands out at either side of head, palms facing in; alternately orbit hands in and away from face

COMPETE

Alternately point thumbs toward and away from chest

Synonym—Race

COMPLAIN

Claw handshape taps middle of chest twice

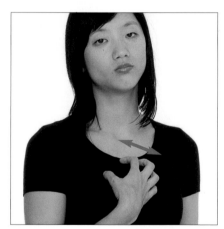

COMPLICATED

Point index fingers at 45 degrees; alternately crook and straighten index fingers while moving hands across each other

COMPUTER
"C" handshape moves up along left forearm twice

CONFLICT
Bring hands together at bases of outstretched index fingers

CONFUSED
Touch head with index finger and rotate claw hands around each other, right over left

CONGRATULATE
Clasp hands together and shake backward and forward twice in front of body

CONNECT

Bring hands together, locking thumbs and index fingers around each other

CONTACT

Brings tips of middle fingers together

CONTINUE

Press right thumb on left and move hands forward in front of chest

CONTROL

Crook index fingers and alternately move hands in and away from body

Synonym—Manage

CONVINCE

Edge of right hand, palm up, strikes left index finger

Synonym—Persuade

COOK

Touch palm of right hand to palm of left hand, then flip right hand over and touch back of right hand against fingers

COOKIE

Mime using a cookie cutter on palm of other hand

COOL (GOOD)

Touch thumb to center of chest and wiggle other fingers

COOL (TEMPERATURE)
Flap fingers up and down over shoulders

COOPERATE
Lock thumbs and index fingers together and rotate hands horizontally in front of chest

COPY
Close fingers while bringing hand to rest on upturned left palm

CORN
Place nail of index finger against lower lip; move finger across bottom lip twice while swiveling hand so that fingernail faces out

CORNER
Place hands at right angles and bring together and tap fingertips together twice

COST
Crook index finger and slide down left palm

Synonym—Price

COUGH
Tap center of chest with clenched fist twice

COUNTRY
Use inside of hand to make circular motions on opposite elbow and lower arm

Synonyms—Nation, rural

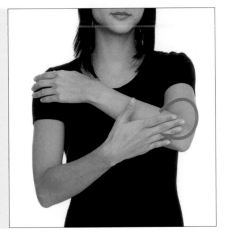 

COUSIN

Make wide cup-shape with hand and swivel hand twice next to head

COW

Touch thumb to side of head, little finger pointing up; twist hand down and back twice

CRAVE

Palm out, thumb folded in; draw index finger down cheek, from above to below lips

Synonym—Desire

CRAZY

Point index finger and
draw circles at side of head

Synonym—Insane

CREATE

Fold thumb in and touch side of
forehead with tip of index finger;
lift hand up and away from self

Synonym—Invent

CRITICIZE

Using index finger, draw small
"X" on left palm

CROSS (VERB)
Sweep upright hand over wrist of left hand, moving in an arc from back to front

CROWDED
Palms together, fingers outstretched, turn hands around while keeping them pressed together

CRY
Touch index fingers to cheeks below eyes; bend index fingers and bring hands down. Repeat motion

 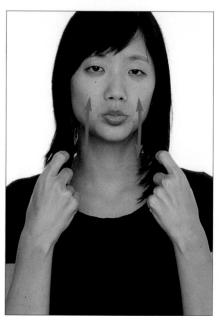

CULTURE

"C" handshape circles once around left index finger, from back to front

CURIOUS

Touch thumb and index finger to throat and shake hand slightly

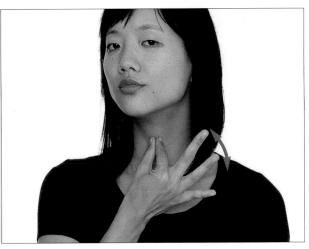

CUTE

Index and middle fingers touch chin, move down and close into hand

From Dance to Duty

DANCE
Swing forked index and middle finger over other palm

DANGEROUS
With thumbs pointing upward and fists clenched, swing outer hand up and bounce knuckles on back of other hand. Repeat motion

DARK
Cross hands, palms in, in front of face

DARN
Snap fingers while swinging hand across body

Synonym—Unfortunately

DAUGHTER
Place fingertips to side of mouth; bring arm down to meet other arm

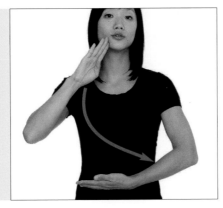 

DAY
Position arms at right angles; stretch out index finger of vertical right arm and swing down to elbow to rest on left arm

DEAD
One palm up, one palm down; rotate hands 180 degrees to reverse position

Synonym—Die

DEAF

Touch index finger to ear and then to side of chin

DECEIVE

Tap folded knuckles of "A" handshape against upright index finger of left hand and pull away

Synonym—Trick

DECIDE

Touch index finger to side of head and bring hand down parallel to other hand; both hands ending side by side in "F" handshape

DECLINE (REFUSE)

Touch index finger to chin; stretch fingers out and bring hand down so that fingers slide out along left palm

Synonym—Refuse

DECREASE
Right "U" handshape turns over and moves down off left "U" handshape

DEEP
Bring down pointing index finger past horizontal left hand

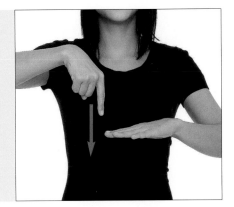

DEFEAT
Clench fists and bend right wrist over the left

Synonym—Beat

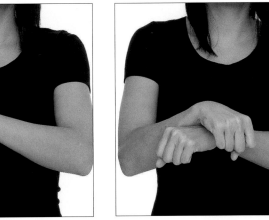

DELETE
Tuck thumb tip under tip of index finger; flick thumb up and out while moving hand up and out

DELICIOUS
Join thumb and middle finger below mouth; bring hand down and slide middle finger back along underside of thumb

DEMOTED
Lower bent hands from side of head

DEODORANT
Mime spraying deodorant under arm

DEPART

Bring hands up and across body
while closing fingers

Synonyms—Go, leave

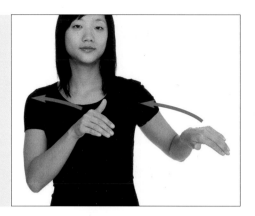

DEPEND ON

Cross index fingers and
push them down twice

Synonym—Rely on

DEPRESSED

Open hands and touch middle
fingers to either side of chest;
slide hands down body

DESPERATE

Alternately rotate middle fingers
in to touch chin in downward
circles

D

DESTROY

Place right hand above left, palms facing, and swipe hands apart while clenching fists

Synonyms—Damage, ruin

DETERIORATE

Thumbs up, at shoulder level; wiggle hands while bringing hands down body

DEVIL

Thumb touches side of head as index and middle finger bend twice

Synonym—Mischievous

DICTIONARY
Strike palm two glancing blows with a "D" handshape

DIFFERENT
Cross index fingers and pull them out and apart

DIFFICULT
Make both index and middle fingers claw shaped; strike side of right hand against side of left

Synonym—Hard

DINNER
Place fingers to mouth; bring fingers down and curve over wrist of arm

DIPLOMA

Hands meet with thumbs and index fingers joined and hands separate

DIRTY

Place back of hand under chin and wiggle fingers

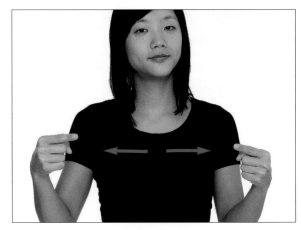

DISAGREE

Touch index finger to side of head; bring both index fingers together then pull apart

DISAPPEAR

Point index finger up between index and middle finger of left hand; bring pointing index finger down and bend finger in

DISCONNECT

Lock thumbs and index fingers together; break chain and separate hands

 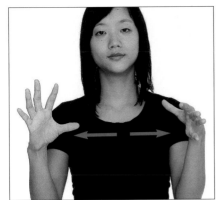

DISCUSS

Tap side of index finger on left palm twice

Synonym—Debate

DISTRIBUTE

Closed hands meet at fingertips; hands spread open while moving out and forward

DIVIDE (MATH)

Edge of right hand touches left, then hands separate out and down

 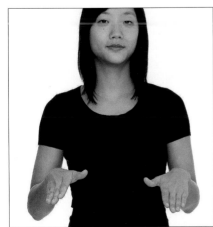

DIVORCE
Clasped hands, right on left, separate out and down, both ending in cupped shape

DOCTOR
Fingers tap inside of left wrist twice

DOESN'T MATTER
Alternately paddle hands toward center of chest, fingertips touching as they pass

DOG
Click finger at side of shoulder then bring hand down to lie flat against hip as though calling a dog

DOLLAR

Clasp left palm between thumb and fingers of right hand and slide right hand along past left fingertips. Repeat motion

DON'T CARE

Touch closed fingers to nose; turn hand away and stretch fingers out in a flicking motion

DON'T KNOW

Place fingers to head and wave hand away

DON'T LIKE

Join thumb and middle finger, touch to chest and bring hand sideways and down, separating thumb and middle finger

Synonym—Dislike

DON'T MIND
Touch index finger to nose, then point finger down and away

 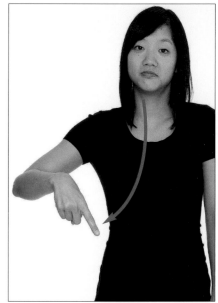

DON'T WANT
Curl fingers inward, then turn hands over, palms down, and bring hands down while uncurling fingers

DOOR
Fold thumbs in and place hands together in upright position, palms out; move right hand away twisting palm in. Repeat motion

D

DOUBT (UNSURE)

Clench fists and alternately move forearms and fists up and down. Repeat motion

DREAM

Touch index finger to side of head; crook index finger while moving hand up and away from head

DRINK

Mime sipping from glass

DRIVE CAR
Simultaneously move fists toward and away from chest. Repeat motion

DROP
Hold fists at chest level, drop fists down and stretch out fingers

DROWN
Extended thumb of fist moves down between index and middle fingers with a slight wiggle

DRUG STORE
Move from "D" handshape to "S" handshape

D

DURING

Move parallel index fingers
forward in a slight down and
up arc

Synonym—While

(GO) DUTCH

Bring clenched fingers toward
each other; as they get closer
stretch out thumbs

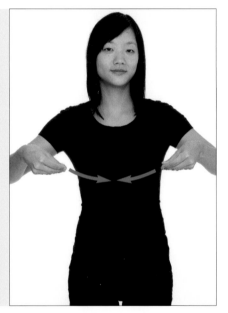

DUTY

Joined fingertips of "D"
handshape tap twice on
left wrist

EACH

With thumbs up, slide right knuckles down base of left thumb

Synonym—Every

EARLY

Touch middle finger to back of left hand; bend finger and move hand forward and down

EARN

Cup hand but keep thumb up; draw hand over palm while closing fingers

Synonym—Collect

EARRINGS

Place tips of thumbs behind earlobes and tips of index fingers on top of earlobes and gently squeeze twice

EARTH

Use thumb and middle finger to clasp left hand; rock right hand backward and forward

EAST

"E" handshape moves to the right

EASY

Fingertips of right hand slap fingertips of left hand twice as they pass by

EAT

Bring fingertips toward mouth

ECSTATIC

Index and middle fingers of right hand jump up and bend from left palm. Repeat motion

Synonym—Delighted

EGG

Index and middle fingers of right hand slide over the index and middle fingers of the left, then move down and away. Repeat motion

EGOTISTICAL

Thumbs and bent index fingers move out sideways from either side of head

Synonym—Conceited

EIGHT
Palm out; bring tips of thumb and middle finger together

EITHER
Wiggle tips of index and middle fingers onto same fingers of left hand

ELECTION
Thumb and index finger mime placing something into top of other clenched hand twice

ELECTRICITY
Crook index fingers and bring knuckles together twice

 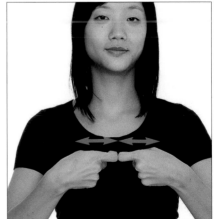

ELEPHANT

Imitate elephant trunk by placing upright hand in front of nose, then sweeping hand down and out

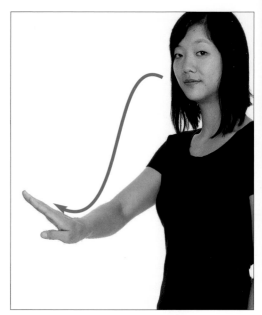

ELEVATOR

"E" handshape slides up and down left palm

EMBARRASSED

Fingers outstretched, palms in; alternately move hands up and down at side of face in slightly circular movements

EMERGENCY
"E" handshape shakes back and
forth a few times

EMOTIONAL
"E" handshapes alternately rotate
outward in front of chest

EMPTY
Middle finger slides across back
of other hand, from
wrist outward

ENCOURAGE
Move hands forward while
rotating them in small
outward circles

END
Right fingertips slide down in front of left fingertips at right angle

ENGAGED (BETROTHED)
"E" handshape makes a small circle down onto back of left ring finger

ENGLAND
Right cupped hand comes down on back of left hand twice

Synonym—English

ENJOY

Rotate both hands against the body, right over left, in opposite circles

Synonym—Appreciate

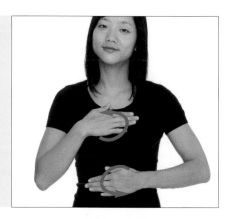 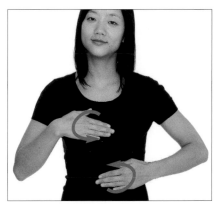

ENOUGH

Right palm slides out across left fist twice

 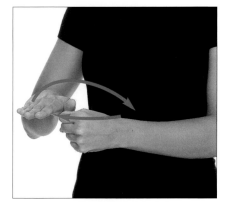

ENTER

Right hand, palm down, slides forward under left

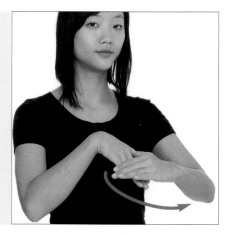 

ENTHUSIASTIC

Rub hands together

Synonym—Eager

EQUAL
Bend fingers and bring tips of both hands together and touch twice

Synonym—Fair

ESCAPE
Slide right index finger outward between index and middle finger of left hand

ESTABLISH
Fist with thumb extended swings up and then down onto back of left hand

EUROPE

Rotate "E" handshape in and bring to side of forehead

EXACT

Place tips of index fingers and thumbs together; rotate right hand and bring down on same joined tips of left hand

EXAGGERATE

Place right fist in front of left; bring right fist away from body in an up/down arc

EXCITED

Point middle fingers in; alternately rotate hands in toward chest, middle fingers touching chest as they pass

EXCUSE

Right fingertips slide out along left palm

Synonym—Forgive

EXCUSE ME

Slide fingertips along left palm twice in short movements

EXERCISE (PHYSICAL)
Raise fists up from shoulders twice

EXPAND
Place right fist on top of left fist; draw hands apart and stretch out fingers

EXPECT
Bend fingers in and down twice with one hand higher

Synonym—Hope

EXPENSIVE
Fingertips move up from left palm, then flick open and down

EXPERIENCE
Fingertips close while sliding down cheek. Repeat motion

EXPERT
Place tip of index finger and thumb together; bring up to chin

EXPLAIN
Place tip of index finger and thumb together on both hands; alternately move hands toward and away from body

Synonym—Describe

EXPRESS
Place fists near each other close to body, then move hands forward, palms up, while stretching open fingers

EYES
Touch index finger to face below right eye and then again below the left

From Face to Future

FACE
Encircle face using index finger

FAIL
"V" handshape slides down and off left palm

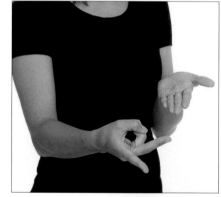

FAINT
Touch forehead with index finger; bring other hand up and sweep hands away to form fists at side of body

FALL ASLEEP

Touch forehead then extend all fingers out and bring hand down to meet other hand, palms in; close eyes and lower head

FALL BEHIND

Right hand moves back toward body from left

FALL DOWN

Stand index and middle finger on left palm; move fingers upward and collapse back of hand onto left palm

FALL IN LOVE

Touch index finger between eyes; bring hand down on left palm and bounce forward to fingertips

FAMILY
"F" handshapes touch at thumb and index finger, then swing out, around and back together

FAMOUS
Touch index fingers at either side of chin; bring hands away from chin in a small arc, and then further away again

FANTASY
"F" handshapes rotate alternately at either side of head

FAR
Point index finger up and out

Synonym—Distant

FARM

Stretch out fingers and slide thumb from left side of chin to the right

FAST

Stretch fingers out in front of body, left hand further forward; draw both hands back quickly and clench fists

Synonym—Quick

FAT

Point hands to either side of waist; bring hands out

FATHER

Tap thumb of open hand on forehead twice

FAULT
Place fingertips on shoulder and hinge hand downward, keeping fingers where they are

FAVORITE
Tap middle finger on chin twice

Synonym—Prefer

FED UP
Lift back of hand to rest under chin

F

FEED

Bring fingertips together on both hands, then push hands forward twice, left hand in front

FEEL

Touch middle finger to center of chest and slide upward

FENCE

With fingers outstretched and thumbs tucked in, pull hands apart

FEW

Bring fingers together, palm facing up, and sweep hand outward and open fingers with the motion

FIGHT
Clench fists and cross arms

FIGURE OUT
"V" handshapes cross at wrists. Repeat motion

FIND
Mime picking something up between thumb and index finger

Synonym—Discover

FINE
Tap center of chest
twice with thumb

Synonym—OK

FINISH
Stretch fingers out, palms facing
in, then sweep hands around so
that palms now face out

Synonym—Already

FIRE (FLAME)
Stretch fingers out, palms in;
alternately move hands up
and down in front of chest
while wiggling fingers

Synonym—Burn

FIRE (FROM JOB)
Swipe back of hand
across top of left fist

113

FIRST
Right index finger moves in to touch extended left thumb

FISH
Touch left fingertips to base of right palm and move right hand back and forth in a fish-tail movement

FISHING
Both hands have crooked index finger touching thumb tip; hold right arm vertical against left hand and flick hand back and forth

FIVE
Stretch out five fingers, palm in

FIX
Fold fingers over thumbs; point both hands together and alternately move into and away from self twice so that fingertips touch while crossing

Synonym—Repair

FLAG
Touch left index finger to wrist of right hand; flap right hand like a flag waving in the breeze

FLATTER

Point left index finger up; swipe fingers of right hand back and forward over the pointing finger

FLEXIBLE

Clasp fingers of left hand between thumb and index finger of right hand; move hand backward and forward, bending left hand to show flexibility

FLIRT

Join thumbs together and bring hands in and out while wiggling fingers

FLOWER
Bring fingertips together and move hand in an arc from one side of nose to other

FOLLOW (TRAIL)
Place right hand behind left and move both forward

FOOTBALL
Bring hands together so that fingers interlock; repeat motion

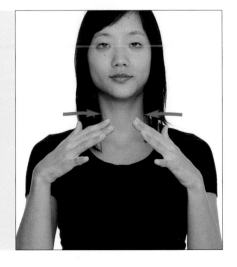

FOR

Index finger touches side of head and twists forward and out

FORBIDDEN

Slap "L" handshape against left palm and pull back smartly

Synonym—Illegal

FORCE

Right hand cup shape bends over left wrist

FOREIGN

"F" handshape rotates on opposite elbow

FOREVER

Index finger touches side of forehead, then becomes "Y" handshape, turns, and moves forward

FORGET

Fingertips move to the right across forehead and close

FORK

Fork index and middle finger into palm twice

FOUR

Raise four fingers, palm in

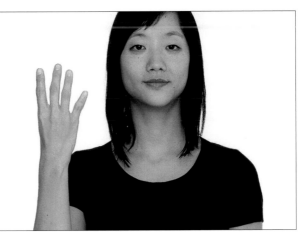

FRANCE

"F" handshape swings inward and to the right

Synonym—French

FREE

"F" handshapes uncross at the wrists and move out

FREEZE

Stretch out hands, palm down; claw fingers in

 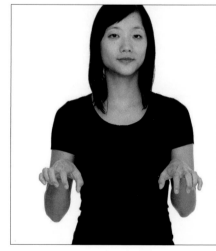

FRENCH FRIES

"F" handshape bobs down and bounces to the right

FRIDAY

Bring index finger and thumb together, palm in, and move in two small, counterclockwise circles from the elbow

FROM

Hold left index finger vertically; crook right index finger and bring in toward body

FRONT

Move palm down in front of face

FRUIT

"F" handshape twists forward and backward on cheek

FRUSTRATED

Hand moves back and backs of fingers tap chin twice

FULL

Swipe palm back and to the left over left fist

Synonym—Fill

FUN

Touch nose with index and middle finger, then swoop them down onto the same fingers on left hand

FUNNY

Flick index and middle finger on the end of the nose twice

FUTURE

Palm moves forward twice from beside right cheek

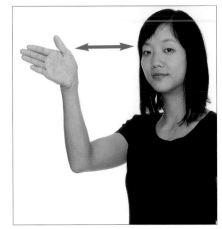

From Gallaudet to Gun

GALLAUDET

Bring index finger and thumb together while moving hand from front to back of head

Note—University for the deaf located in Washington, D.C. Thomas Hopkins Gallaudet, its founder

GAME

Raise thumbs and bring knuckles together twice

Synonym—Sports

GARAGE

Stretch out thumb, index, and middle finger; move hand in, out, and in under left palm

GENERAL

Bring tips of fingers together in "V" shape, palms in; flap hands apart, palms out

GERMANY

Cross hands at wrist and wiggle fingers

Synonym—German

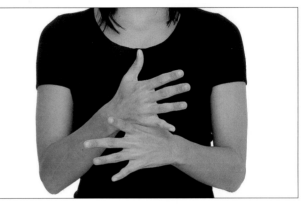

GET (ACQUIRE)

Open hands move back and into fists, right hand on left

Synonyms—Acquire, obtain, receive, procure

GET IN

Claw index and middle fingers; move into cupped hand

GET ON
Fork index and middle finger and wedge up and over fingers of left hand

GET UP
Forked index and middle fingers come up and then down to "stand" on left palm

GIRAFFE
Cup hand in front of neck, then raise hand up to top of head

GIRL
Brush side of jaw with inside of thumb twice

Synonym—Female

GIVE
Closed handshape moves up,
forward, and down

GIVE IN
Place palm against chest;
bring hand out, palm facing up

GLASS
Crook index finger and
tap teeth twice

GO
Index fingers move forward
and decline to horizontal

GOD
Flat hand moves down to rest vertically near chin

GOLF
Index fingers crook to meet thumbs and hands; swing right to left as in a golf stroke

GOOD
Fingertips move down and forward from chin

GOSSIP

Open and close thumbs and index fingers while moving hands in counterclockwise horizontal circles from mouth

Synonym—Rumor

GOVERNMENT

Index finger bends, turns toward head, and straightens against temple

GRADUATE

Drop "G" handshape down onto left palm

GRANDFATHER

Thumb of open hand touches forehead and moves down and out in two small arc motions

GRANDMOTHER

Thumb of open hand touches chin and moves down and out in two small arc motions

GREEDY

Clench hand against chin and pull down into fist

Synonym—Selfish

GREEN

Swing "G" handshape in two short arcs near shoulder

GRIEF

Bring fists together near heart and wring one hand down, one hand up in a twisting motion

Synonyms—Agony, misery

GROUP

Open claw hands to circle around invisible ball

GROW

Closed right hand moves up and opens from inside cupped left hand

GROW UP
Horizontal hand moves
up near shoulder

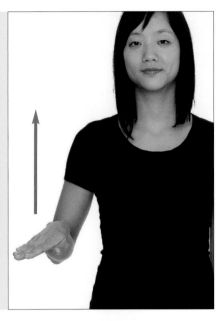

GUILTY
"G" handshape taps left
shoulder twice

GULLIBLE
Bring back of wrist to forehead
and flap middle three fingers
down to palm twice

Synonym—Naive

GUN
Point index and middle fingers
and wiggle thumb

From Habit to Husband

HABIT

Right hand crosses onto left at wrist; hands lower and close to fists

Synonym—Tendency

HAIR

Thumb and index finger move out from side of head twice

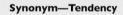

HAMBURGER

Clasp hands; swap position of hands and clasp again

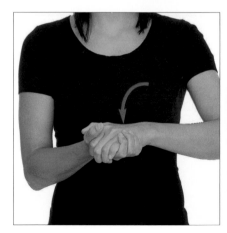

HANDS

Slide edge of right hand in across wrist of left hand and repeat action with hands reversed

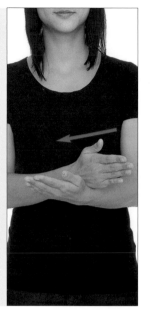
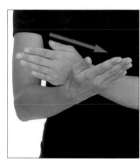

HANDSOME

Move hand outward from chin, then describe a circle around face with index finger

HANGER

Hooked right index finger bounces twice, left to right, along left index finger

HAPPEN

Palms up, point index fingers and raise hands; lower hands while turning palm down

Synonym—Occur

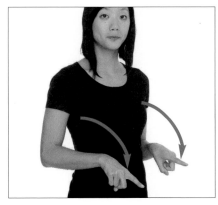

HAPPY

Hand describes two upward and outward circles, touching chest as it passes

Synonyms—Pleased, lighthearted, contented, glad

HARD (SOLID)

Raise fists and bring knuckles down on back of left hand twice

Synonym—Solid

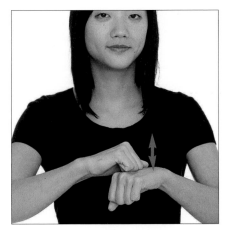

HARD OF HEARING

Index and middle finger handshape moves down and bounces once to the right

HAT
Pat top of head twice

HATE
Flick middle fingers
out from thumbs

HAVE
Bent hands move in to
touch either side of
chest with fingertips

Synonyms—Possess, own

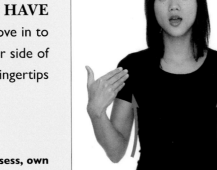 

HE
Point with index finger

Synonyms—She, it, there

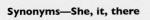

HEAD
Bent handshape fingertips touch side of head and then side of chin

HEAR
Touch ear with index finger

HEARING AID
Hook index finger around ear and tap down twice

HEART
Tap twice at heart with middle finger

HEAVEN
Hands rotate around each other and come to rest at either sides of head

HEAVY
Lower open hands

HELL
"H" handshape slides diagonally down from left to right

HELLO
Hand moves out from forehead

HELP
Place right fist, thumb up, on left palm and raise both hands

HERE
Place hands, palms up, at either side of body; bring hands in and out using a circular motion

HIDE
Back of thumb moves down from
mouth to hide under left palm

HIGH
"H" handshape moves up
at side of body

HIGH SCHOOL
"H" to "S" handshape

HIGHWAY
Point index and middle fingers
across body and then move
hands across each other twice

HIRE
Palm up, bring hand in
toward center of body

Synonym—Invite

HIS
Move hand in direction of person

Synonym—Her

HISTORY
Move "H" handshape down twice

HOCKEY
Sweep knuckle of crooked index finger down onto palm of other hand. Repeat motion

HOLD
Clench fist and shake hand in front of shoulder

HOLY
"H" handshape moves to base of palm of upturned left hand, turns over and changes to flat hand, and slides out across left palm

HOME

Closed fingers touch side of lower and then upper cheek

HONEST

"H" handshape middle finger slides out along left palm

Synonym—Truth

HONOR

Position left "H" handshape ahead of the right; bring hands down and out from body

HORSE

Touch thumb to side of head and bend index and middle fingers down twice

HOSPITAL
Fingers of "H" handshape draw cross on side of left shoulder

HOT
Claw handshape turns out and moves down from mouth

Synonym—Heat

HOUR
Point right index finger up and rest knuckles on inside of left hand; rotate the hand right around palm once

HOUSE
Form inverted "V" with hands; draw hands apart and then down to imitate outline of roof and sides of house

HOW
Palms down touching in front of chest with fingers at right angles to palms; curl hands out so that thumbs point forward

HOW MANY
Raise and open fists

HUMBLE
Place side of right index finger at mouth, then lower hand and point fingertips at left palm from underneath

Synonym—Modest

HUMID
Close thumb and middle fingers while moving hands down and repeat without stopping

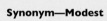

HUNGRY
Slide "C" handshape down chest

HURRY
"H" handshape moves up
and down twice

Synonym—Rush

HURT
Point index fingers together, with
one palm facing down, the other
facing up; rotate both hands so
the positions are reversed

Synonym—Injure

HUSBAND
Touch thumb of open hand on
forehead and move down
to clasp left hand

I
Point to center of chest
with index finger

Synonym—Me

ICE CREAM
Move fist toward mouth as if
holding an ice cream cone, then
down and back in a small circle.
Repeat motion

IDEA
Tip of little finger touches side of
forehead and hand moves up
and out

Synonym—Concept

IF
"I" handshape moves to
"F" handshape

IGNORE
Palm in, fingers extended; touch
nose with index finger and move
hand down to the left

Synonym—Neglect

IMPATIENT
Hook index and middle
finger and rock hand back and
forth across the back of
left hand. Repeat motion

**Synonyms—Restless, anxious,
edgy, agitated**

IMPORTANT
Point thumbs and index fingers together; raise hands, bringing hands out and back in together

IMPOSSIBLE
"Y" handshape hits left palm. Repeat motion

IMPROVE
Edge of right hand bounces twice up left forearm

IN
Dip five fingers into cupped hand

INCLUDE

Stretch fingers to the side, then bring together and insert into cupped hand

INCOMPETENT

Extend right fingers downward, grip thumb with left hand and twist right hand up so that palm faces out

INCREASE

Right "U" handshape rises and turns over to rest on left "U" handshape fingers

INDIA

Extended thumb twists twice while pressing middle of forehead

INDIVIDUAL
Place hands in front of chest, little fingers pointing out, and lower hands

INFLUENCE
Closed handshape opens and moves forward from back of left hand

INFORM
Point fingers together, right hand touching forehead, left in front of face; bring hands out and away from body while opening fingers

INNOCENT
Touch index and middle fingers of each hand to sides of chin at 45 degrees and move hands down and away from chin

INSPIRED
Touch fingers to chest; raise hands and open fingers

INSULT
Point index finger out, then up and forward

Synonym—Offend

INTERESTING

With palms in, right hand on top, thumbs and middle fingers near body, draw hands out while drawing thumbs and middle fingers together

INTERMISSION

Wedge fingers sideways between index and middle finger of left hand

INTERRUPT

Push hand forward and down between thumb and index finger of edge of left hand

INTERVIEW
Point little fingers up and alternately move hands toward and away from chest

INTRODUCE
Palms facing up, point fingers across body, both arms wide apart; bring hands close together

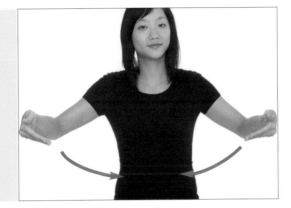 

IRELAND
Hook middle and index fingers, circle and bring down on back of hand

ITALY
Little finger describes a cross in front of forehead

JAIL

Backs of spread right fingers tap forward twice against spread left fingers

Synonym—Prison

JAPAN

Join hands using tips of thumbs and index fingers; pull hands apart while closing fingers and repeat

Synonym—Japanese

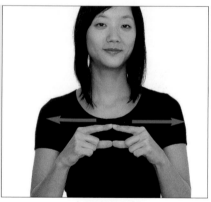

JEALOUS

Touch crooked index finger to side of mouth; turn finger round to point backward

JEWISH
Close fingers together while drawing them down chin. Repeat motion

JUMP
Stand right index and middle finger on left palm; lift and bend fingers then bring down again with fingers straightened

From Keep to Know

KEEP
Right "V" handshape moves down onto left

KEY
Rotate knuckle of right index finger forward against left palm. Repeat motion

KICK

Using chopping motion, bring right hand up to strike left hand from below

KILL

Point index finger down at 45 degrees and slide hand under left palm

KIND

Palms in, rotate hands around each other in an outward circular motion

Synonyms—Generous, gentle

159

KISS
Closed fingertips touch together and then separate

KITCHEN
"K" handshape turns over on left palm

KNEEL
Stand knuckles of index and middle finger on left palm

KNIFE
Swipe right index finger down across left as though sharpening a knife. Repeat motion

KNOW
Tap side of forehead twice with fingertips together

 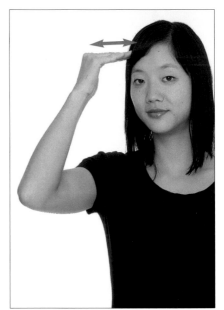

LAMP

Place fingers together pointing down, then open fingers

Synonym—Light

LANGUAGE

"L" handshapes meet at thumbs and separate as hands twist down and out slightly

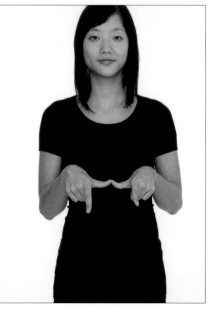

LAST (FINAL)
Right little finger touches left as it moves down at a right angle

LATE (NOT ON TIME)
Palm points down and waves back twice

LATER
Place thumb on left palm and point index finger up; twist thumb so index finger swivels forward and down

LAUGH
Point both index fingers and brush outward and back from cheeks. Repeat motion

LAW
Place right "L" handshape against left palm and bounce down once

LAZY
Tap left shoulder twice with "L" handshape

LEAD (GUIDE)

Clasp fingers of left hand and pull hands away from body

LEARN

Spread fingers and rest on other palm; lift hand and bring fingers together on forehead

LEAVE (BEHIND)

Move open hands forward and down

LECTURE
Move hand forward and down twice from wrist

Synonym—Speech

LESSON
Bounce bent hand down left palm with one hand from fingertips to base of palm

LETTER
Point thumb to lips then bring down on inside of left fingers

Synonym—Mail

LIBRARY

Move "L" handshape in two small clockwise circles in front of shoulder

LICENSE

Thumbs of "L" handshapes tap together twice

LIE

Move bent handshape to the left under chin

LIE DOWN

Fork middle and index finger and draw back toward body across left palm

LIGHT (WEIGHT)

Point middle fingers in; turn hands so that middle fingers point up

 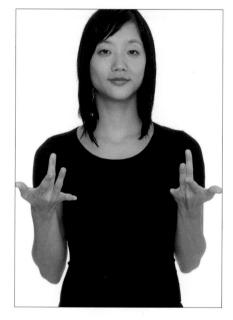

LIGHTNING

Index finger moves downward in zigzag motion

LIKE

Thumb and middle fingers touch chest and close as hand moves forward

LIMIT

With both bent handshapes pointing in, right over left, swivel hands at 90 degrees outward

LINE OF WORK

Slide fingers across top of left hand held from back of index finger forward

Synonyms—Major (academic), profession

 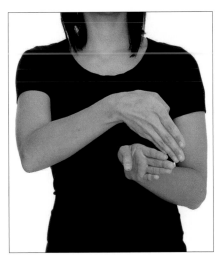

LIST (NOUN)
Tap inside of hand three times from left fingertips down left palm

LISTEN
Place thumb of cup-shaped hand at ear

LITTLE BIT
Knuckles facing out, rub tips of thumb and index finger together

LIVE
Fists with thumbs extended slide
up body

Synonym—Life

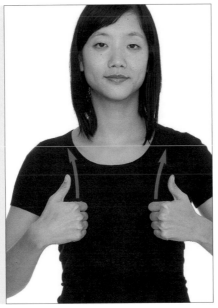 

LOCKED
Right fist swivels to palm up
and lowers onto back of left
fist, wrist on wrist

LONDON
Index finger of "L" handshape moves in two forward
circles near temple

LONELY

Move index finger in two circles; touch chin, then down, forward and out. Move index finger back up and down across chin again

LONG

Draw index finger from left wrist to elbow

LOOK AT

Fork index and middle finger and move hand outward from face

Synonym—Watch

LOOK FOR

Cup hand and rotate in two counterclockwise circles in front of face

Synonym—Search

LOS ANGELES

"L" to "A" handshape in front of body. Repeat motion

LOSE (COMPETITION)

Index and middle finger handshape lowers on to left palm

LOSE (MISPLACE)

Curl fingers in to join hands at knuckles; draw hands apart and out while spreading fingers

LOUSY

Stretch out thumb, index, and middle finger ("3" handshape), touch thumb to nose and bring hand right, left, and down

Synonyms—Awful, terrible

LOVE

Fists move into body crossing at wrists

LOW
Flat hand moves down twice

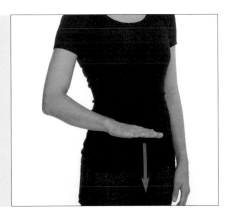 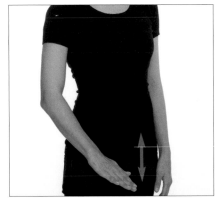

LUCKY
Middle finger touches chin and flicks down

Synonym—Fortunate

LUGGAGE
Bend arm and clench fist, as if carrying a suitcase; lift hand up and down twice

Synonym—Suitcase

LUNCH
Bring tips of fingers to mouth; straighten arm so that fingers point up and rest elbow on back of left hand

MACHINE
Join hands together at
knuckles to form "cog";
rock hands up and down

Synonyms—Factory, motor

MAGAZINE
Slide thumb and knuckles
up and down side of
left hand twice

MAGIC

Curl fingers in to form fists in front of shoulders; move hands out, palms down, and spread fingers

MAKE (PRODUCE)

Place right fist on left, knuckles out; twist hands in, knuckles toward self

MAN

Thumb of open hand touches forehead and moves down to chest

MANY
Fists open as hands lower

MARCH
Stretch fingers and point tips down, left hand in front of the right; brush both hands backward and forward

Synonym—Parade

MARRY
Start with hands apart, right higher than the left, and bring together in a clasp

MATCH (FIRE)
Bring thumb and side of index finger together; place on palm of left hand and flick up as if striking a match

MATCH (FIT)
Bring knuckles together so hands interlock

MATH
"M" handshapes move sideways so that they rub across each other twice

 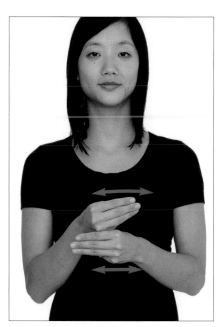

MAXIMUM

Bring back of right hand up to meet palm of left hand

MAYBE

Palms up, alternately raise and lower hands at either side of body

Synonym—Probably

MEAN (NASTY)

Touch nose with index finger, other fingers outstretched; bring hand down, curling in fingers to form fist, and strike past knuckles of left hand

Synonyms—Cruel, nasty

MEANING

Fork index and middle finger into palm; lift and twist fingers round so that back of hand faces out

MEASURE

Bring tips of thumbs together and point out little fingers; tap thumbs together twice

MEAT

Clasp hand, palm in, between thumb and index finger of right hand; shake hands slightly

MECHANIC
Swivel index and middle finger
around left index finger

Synonym—Plumber

MEDICINE
Touch middle finger to left palm and
rock hand from side to side

MEET
Point index fingers up and
bring hands together

MEETING

Join hands by bringing thumbs together; fold fingers in so that tips touch twice

Synonym—Conference

MELT

Adjacent hands change from "O" to "A" handshapes as hands separate

Synonym—Dissolve

MEMORIZE

Place fingertips on forehead and bring hand out to form fist

MEXICO
Index finger of fork handshape touches forehead above right eye, then flicks down twice

MICROSCOPE
Tilt head down at an angle to look through cupped hands, right on top of the left; swivel hands back and forth as if adjusting magnification

MICROWAVE OVEN
Point fists at each other, and open and close fingers

MIDDLE

Extended middle finger rotates
and lowers to rest on left palm

Synonym—Center

MILITARY

With right hand higher than
the left, tap knuckles against
left side of chest twice

MILK

Close fist twice

MINIMUM

Right fingertips rise up from
on top of left fingertips

MINUTE

Right index finger clicks forward
with hand against left palm

MISS
(FAIL TO CATCH)

Wide cup-shape sweeps down
across face and closes to fist

Synonym—Guess

MISS
(WISH TO SEE)
Touch index finger up to chin

Synonym—Disappointed

MISTAKE
Spread thumb and little
finger; wrap knuckles
against chin twice

Synonym—Error

MOCK (RIDICULE)
Point index and little
finger out on both hands;
jab hands forward twice

Synonym—Ridicule

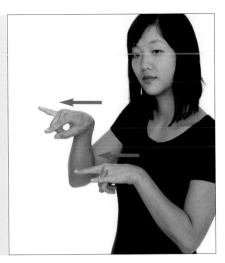

MONDAY

"M" handshape, fingers pointing upward; make two small horizontal counterclockwise circles

MONEY

Tap back of closed handshape on palm twice

MONTH

Back of right index finger slides down side of left index finger

MOON

Form a half-round shape with thumb and index finger around eye; move hand up and out

MORE

Tap fingertips of each hand together twice

MORNING

Rest left hand inside right elbow; raise right arm from elbow

MOSQUITO
Touch thumb and index
finger to cheek, then move
hand out and slap palm
against cheek

Synonym—Bee

MOST
Bring right "A" handshape
up past left

MOTHER
Tap chin twice with thumb
of open hand

MOTORCYCLE
Mime clutching handlebars; move knuckles of right hand backward and forward as though revving the engine

MOUNTAIN
Wrap back of left hand with knuckles; raise both hands at same angle with fingers outstretched

MOUSE
Skim nose with index finger by moving hand across front of face twice

MOVE (FROM/TO)
Closed handshapes
move out in an arc

MOVIE
With fingers stretched, palm
facing out and hand resting
on back of other hand, make a
few waving motions

Synonym—Video

MUSIC
Sweep fingers backward and
forward over left arm

MUST
Hook index finger and bring hand down

Synonym—Have to

MY
Press center of chest, palm facing in

MYSELF
Thumb raised, press knuckles against center of chest twice

NAME
Tap index and middle finger twice at a right angle on same fingers of left hand

NAPKIN
Rotate fingertips counterclockwise in front of mouth

NEAR

Move back of right hand forward to palm of left hand

Synonym—Close (by)

NEAT (GOOD)

Bend thumb and index finger together and place on side of cheek; twist hand forward

NEGATIVE (ADJECTIVE)

Tap side of index finger against other palm twice

NEPHEW
Place index and middle finger handshape next to side of head and swivel hand back and forth

NERVOUS
Spread fingers and shake hands at either side of body

NEVER
With palm starting at 45 degrees, swerve hand to right, then down

NEW

With fingers bent in, strike knuckles across left palm

NEW YORK

Point thumb and little finger and strike knuckles back and forth across other palm

NEWSPAPER

Bring back of thumb down on left palm while bringing index finger to thumb, and repeat

NEXT (IN ORDER)
Lift right hand up and over left hand

NEXT (TO)
Place right palm against left hand; move right hand to the right in a slight arc

Synonym—Neighbor

NICE
Wipe right palm across left palm

NIECE

Place index and middle finger handshape next to chin and swivel hand back and forth

NIGHT

Bend fingers at right angle to palm; lower hand onto left wrist and bounce once

Synonym—Evening

NINE

Bring tips of thumb and index finger together; palm out, other fingers raised

NO
Thumb, index, and middle
fingers close together

NONE
Closed handshapes move
out and down

Synonym—Nothing

NORTH
"N" handshape moves up

NOSEY
Tap nose twice with tip
of index finger

NOT
Place thumb behind tip of
chin and bring forward
and slightly down

Synonym—Don't

NOT YET
Swing hand back twice
from the wrist

NOTHING
Fist moves down and forward while opening

NOTICE
Crook index finger and touch cheek below eye; bring finger down to left palm

Synonym—Recognize

NOW
Stretch out thumbs and little fingers and lower hands twice

NUMBER

Join hands by bringing fingertips together, one palm down, one up; swivel hands so that the palm positions are reversed

NURSE

Tap fingertips of "N" handshape twice against inside of left wrist

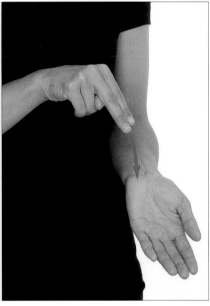 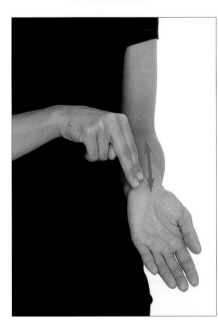

OCCUR (TO)

Index finger touches side of forehead and swings down to rise up between index and middle finger of left hand

Synonym—Realize

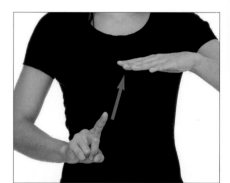

OF COURSE

Slap index and middle finger down on back of left hand

OFFER
Palms rise up and away
from body

Synonym—Suggest

OFTEN
Bounce fingertips a few times
out along palm of left hand

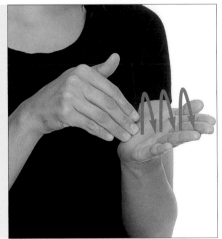 

Synonym—Frequently

OH, I SEE
Spread thumb and little
finger; rock hand up and
down from elbow

OLD

Claw hand under chin; swerve hand down to chest then straight down to waist while curling fingers to form fist

ONCE

Flick index finger up from palm of left hand

ONE

Palm in, raise index finger

ONION
Touch crooked index finger
next to eye and swivel twice

ONLY
Point index finger up, palm
out; twist hand down and to
the left and back up with
palm in

OPEN
Brings hands together,
palms down; separate hands
and turn palms over

OPEN MINDED

Cover forehead with fingers and swing both hands out

Synonym—Liberal

OPINION

With fingertips together, pivoting from the wrist, slightly rock hand back and forth next to forehead

OPPORTUNITY

Move hands forward, changing handshapes from "O" to "K"

OPPOSITE
Pull tips of index fingers apart

ORANGE
Clench fist twice
in front of mouth

OTHER
Point thumb to the left and
rotate up over to the right

Synonym—Another

OUR

Cup hand with thumb against chest; arc hand across body so that little finger rests against left side of chest

OUT

Lift closed hand out from cupped hand

OVERHEAR

Place thumb to side of ear; curl index and middle fingers twice

Synonym—Eavesdrop

OVERLOOK
With palm in, wave hand down
in front of face

Synonym—Miss (don't notice)

OWE
Point index finger down
at 45 degrees and tap
left palm twice

**Synonyms—Afford, due,
payable, unpaid, debt**

From Paint to Puzzled

PAINT
(LARGE SURFACE)
Sweep hand up and down from wrist as though it were a paintbrush

PAPER
Strike right palm down and across left palm twice

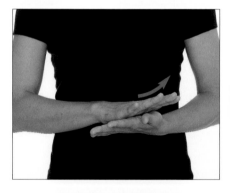
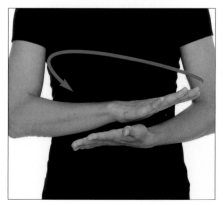

PARIS
Move index and middle fingers up to join at tips

PARKING
Stretch thumb, index and middle finger; bring hand down onto left palm twice

PARTICIPATE
Insert index and middle fingers into clenched left hand

Synonym—Join

PARTY
"Y" handshapes swivel
down and back twice

PASS
Thumbs up, knuckles out; move
right hand ahead of the left

PAST
Move hand back over shoulder
and bend at wrist

Synonyms—Previous, former

PATIENT (ADJECTIVE)
Thumb up, knuckles facing out; bring hand down from nose to chin twice

Synonym—Tolerant

PAY
Flick out index finger from left palm

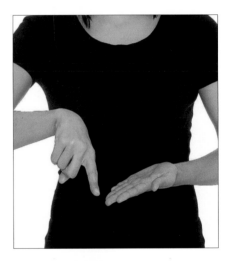

PAY ATTENTION
Place hands at side of head, palms facing in; move hands forward and down

Synonym—Concentrate

PEACE

Bring hands up so that insides of fingers meet, then swivel hands 45 degrees and lower and separate them

PEOPLE

Use "P" handshapes to make small alternating circles

PERFECT

Bring index finger and thumb together on both hands; circle right hand and bring tips of fingers down to lower hand

PERSON
Move horizontal "P" handshapes down

PERSONALITY
Make small circle with "P" handshape and bring to left shoulder

PHILOSOPHY
Swivel "P" handshape down twice at forehead

PHOTOCOPY

Spread right fingers up so tips rest on left palm; bring right hand down while closing fingers together

Synonyms—Xerox, copy

PHYSICS

Crooked middle and index fingers come together and touch twice

PICK ON

Bring thumb and tip of index finger together; tap down on vertical left index finger twice

Synonym—Harass

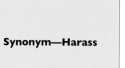

PICTURE

Cup hand at side of face; bring down and place against left palm

Synonym—Photograph

PIE

Slide edge of hand diagonally across left palm; repeat, sliding across at a different angle as though cutting a pie

PINK

Stroke middle finger of "P" handshape down chin twice

PITY

Point middle fingers down and rotate hands outward and back. Repeat motion

Synonym—Sympathy

PIZZA

Spread thumbs and index fingers as if holding a pizza; twist hands up and down twice

PLACE (LOCATION)

Touch middle fingers of "P" handshape in front of body; separate them, move them back, then bring them together again

PLAN
Point hands out at either side of body, palms facing in; sway both hands down and up again to the right

Synonym—Organize

PLANT
Right hand opens as it moves up from inside left hand

Synonym—Spring (noun)

PLAY (FUN)
With thumbs and little fingers raised, rotate both hands out and back twice

PLEASE

Hand rotates counterclockwise on chest

POLICE

Cup hand and tap twice against left shoulder

POLITE

Thumb gently strikes center of chest in the upward movement of each of two small up-and-out circles

POLITICS

Middle finger of "P" handshape turns over and moves in to touch temple

PONDER

Fingers wiggle together as hand rotates at side of forehead

Synonym—Consider

POOR

Clasp left elbow with fingertips of right hand; immediately pull down and repeat

223

POPCORN
Alternately raise and lower hands, extending index fingers on the way up and retracting them on the way down

POPULAR
Tap palm twice against side of vertically held index finger of left hand

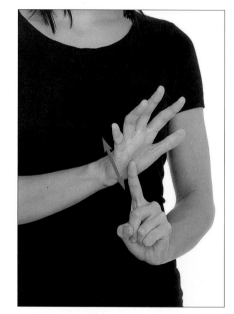

POSITIVE
Tap side of horizontal index finger twice against side of upright index finger of left hand

POSSIBLE
Clench fists, knuckles out; rock hands up and down twice

POTATO
Crook index and middle finger and tap twice on back of other hand

POWERFUL
Make wide cup shape with hand; tap against biceps of left arm and bring back out

Synonym—Strong

PRACTICE (REHEARSE)
Rub knuckles back and forth along index finger of other hand

Synonym—Train (practice)

P

PRAY

Move praying hands in an inward circular motion

PREDICT

Bring index and middle fingers close to face, then under and past left palm

PREFER

Tap middle finger twice on chin

PREGNANT

Spread fingers and place palm on abdomen; bring hand outward

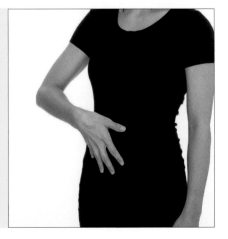 

PRESIDENT

Bring hands together in front of face, palms facing out; move hands apart and curl fingers in to form fists

Synonym—Superintendent

PRETEND

Place right palm on top of left; dip fingers forward

Synonyms—Fake, hypocrite

PRETTY

Open fingers at side of face; bring hand down past face while moving fingers together and swivel hand

Synonym—Beautiful

PREVENT

Cross right hand behind left and push out

PROBLEM
Bring knuckles of index and middle fingers together and twist hands

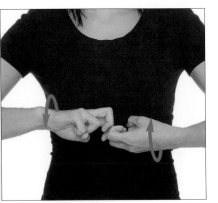 

PROCEED
Place hands apart, palms in, and point fingers toward each other; move hands forward

PROCESS
Rotate hands around each other in a forward circular motion

PROFIT
Slide side of index finger and thumb together down torso

Synonym—Benefit

228

P

PROMISE
Bring side of index finger to lips; lower hand so that palm rests on left fist

Synonym—Guarantee

PROMOTED
Place hands parallel at chest level, fingers bent toward each other; raise hands using a slight inward arc

PROTESTANT
Bent index and middle fingers come down twice on left palm

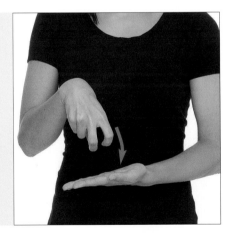 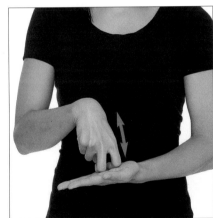

PROUD
Thumb slides up torso

229

PROVE
Bring back of hand to opposite palm and bounce back up

PUNISH
Strike a glancing blow against the left elbow with the right forefinger

PURPLE
Swing "P" handshape in two short arcs near shoulder with wrist bent forward

PUT

Bring fingers of each hand
together; lift and move both
hands out and down again

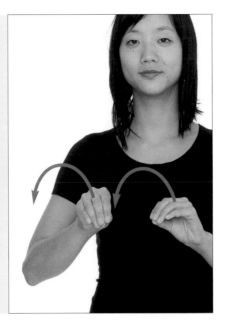

PUZZLED

Point index finger out,
crook finger, and bring
back against forehead

QUARREL

Index fingers alternately move
up and down at each other

Synonym—Argue

QUIET

Cross edge of right hand in
front of mouth; bring hands
out and down

QUIT
Right index and middle fingers
pull out of left fist

Synonym—Resign

RABBIT
Cross arms at wrists, palms in; fold in index and middle fingers twice

RAIN
Move claw hands up and down twice from wrist

READ
Point index and middle fingers at palm and sweep down twice from wrists

 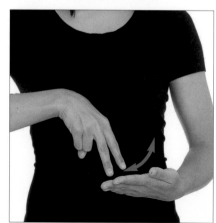

READY
Move parallel "R" handshapes from left to right

REAL
Place side of index finger on chin; immediately bring hand forward and down

Synonyms—Really, true, sure

REASON
"R" handshape describes two small outward circles next to forehead

RECENTLY
Crook index finger twice on lower cheek

Synonym—Lately

235

RED
Crook finger twice from chin

REDUCE
Right index finger moves down
near upturned left index finger

Synonym—Decrease

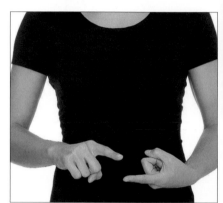

REFUSE
Raise thumb and bring
straight back over shoulder

REGULAR
Point index fingers diagonally
out and tap hands together twice

Synonyms—Typical, usual

REJECT
Point thumb up then twist
hand around to point down

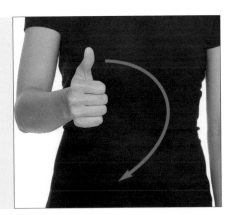

RELIEVED
Hands slide down torso

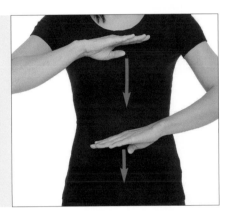

RELIGION
Touch tip of "R" handshape to
left shoulder; swing down
and forward

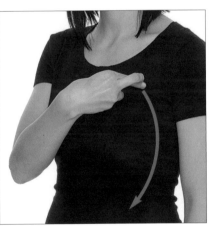

REMEMBER
Right thumb moves down from side of forehead
to rest on back of other thumb and
bounces once

237

R
RESENT • RESIGN • RESIST • RESPONSIBILITY

RESENT
Thumb flicks upward off of chest

RESIGN
Move bent index and middle fingers up and out to the side of cupped left hand

Synonym—Quit

RESIST
Horizontal forearm and fist move away from body

Synonyms—Defend, resent, withstand

RESPONSIBILITY
Place fingertips of both hands on right shoulder and press down

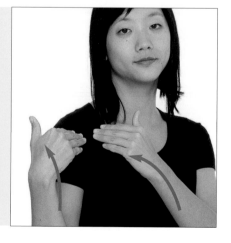

238

R

REST

Cross wrists in front of chest, palms facing in; tap hands twice against chest

Synonym—Relax

RESTAURANT

Touch fingertips of "R" handshape to one side of mouth and move to other

RESTROOM

"T" handshape shakes sideways, back and forth

Synonyms—Bathroom, toilet

RETIRE (FROM WORK)

Stretch both hands in front of chest so that fingertips face each other; bring thumbs in to chest

REVENGE (GET)

With tips of bent index finger and thumb together on each hand, bring right hand up to touch the left

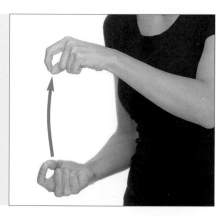
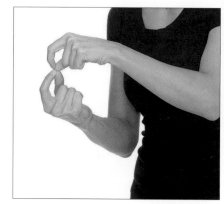

RICH

Raise back of closed hand up from left palm and open

Synonym—Wealthy

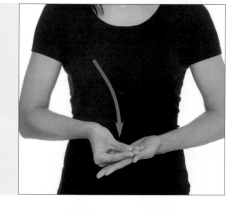

RIDE IN

Hook index and middle finger over thumb of cupped left hand; use thumb to pull right hand forward

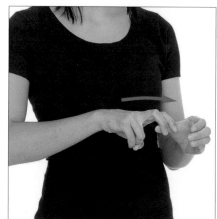

RIDE ON

Fork middle and index finger over edge of left hand; move hands forward

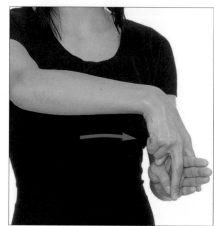

RIGHT (CORRECT)

Point index fingers diagonally out; bring right hand down onto left hand

Synonyms—Correct, proper, appropriate

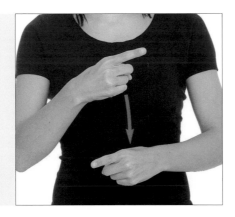

RIGHT (ENTITLEMENT)

Swivel right hand up on left palm

RIVER

Touch index finger of "W" handshape to chin; lower hand and then move both hands forward, right behind left, with fingers outstretched and wiggling

ROOM

Place bent right hand in front of bent left; move hands round so that palms face each other

Synonym—Box

ROOMMATE

Fold fingers in and bring
hands together so that
knuckles interlock; repeat

ROUGH

Make hand claw shaped;
brush fingernails out
over other palm twice

RUDE

Brush middle finger
out over other palm

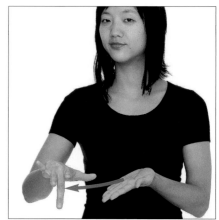

RUIN

Crook index fingers; skim
right hand out over left hand

Synonym—Spoil

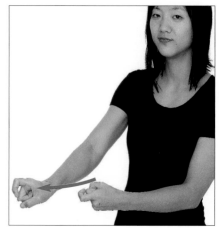

RULE (POLICY)
Bounce fingertips of "R" handshape once down left palm

RUN (EXERCISE)
Thumbs up, hook left index finger around thumb of right hand in front; push both hands out while crooking right index finger

RUSSIA
Side of index finger slides to the right along chin and moves down

SAD
Open hands and lower from face

SAFE (PROTECTED)
Cross wrists, left over right, fists clenched in; uncross arms and rotate them out and down

Synonyms—Save, rescue

SAME
Bring index fingers to meet horizontally, side by side

SAN FRANCISCO, CA

"S" to "F" handshapes

SANDWICH

Fold fingers of right hand
over left, palms in; bring
fingertips toward mouth twice

Synonym—Picnic

SATISFIED

Right hand above the
left, palms down;
bring hands to body

Synonym—Content

SATURDAY

Fist clenched, rotate hand using
left-to-right inward circling motion

SAVE (KEEP)

Form "scissors" with index and middle fingers; bring right hand down on left hand

Synonym—Keep

SAY

Tap index finger twice on chin

SCHOOL

Bring right palm down onto left palm twice

SCIENCE

Stick thumbs out so they face each other; alternately rotate hands in and around

SCOLD
Wag index finger back and forward a few times

SECRET
Tap lips twice with thumbnail

Synonyms—Private, confidential

SECRETARY
Touch index and middle fingers to upper cheek; bring fingers down and slide out across other palm

SEE
Touch middle finger of "V" handshape to cheek near eye; bring hand forward

SEEM

Twist slightly curved hand backward and forward at side of head twice

Synonym—Apparently

 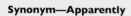

SELFISH

Spread index and middle fingers and point out; bring hands in while hooking index and middle fingers under

Synonym—Greedy

 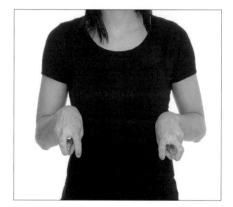

SEMESTER

Fist near left shoulder moves to the right and down

SEND

Brush fingertips out over back of left hand

SENSITIVE

Touch middle finger to chest; flick finger slightly up and bring hand out and down

SENTENCE

Bring index fingers and thumbs together so that both hands are joined; move right hand away

Synonym—Language

SEPARATE

Touch backs of fingers together and pull them apart

SERIOUS

Touch index finger to chin and twist

SEVEN
With palm out, touch tip of
ring finger to tip of thumb

SEVERAL
Arc hand out in front of body
while opening fingers;
keep thumb tucked in

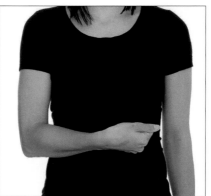 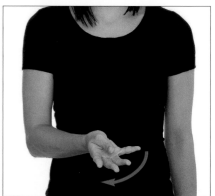

SHIRT
Grasp shirt near right shoulder with thumb and
index finger; pull forward slightly twice

SHOCKED
Touch forehead with index
finger; lower hand so that
both hands face down in
slight claw shape

SHOES
Clench fists and knock
together twice

 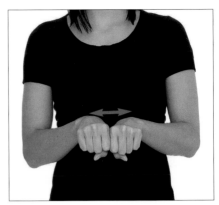

SHOPPING
Bring fingers together and
brush out over other palm twice

 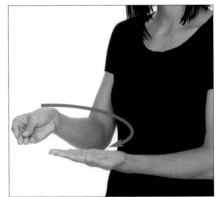

SHORT (HEIGHT)
Bent handshape bounces
down twice

SHORT (TIME)
Right index and middle fingers
touch those of the left hand and
move back and forth twice

Synonym—Brief, soon

SHOULD

Hook index finger and move hand down twice

Synonym—Ought to

SHOUT

Claw fingers and bring to mouth; bring fingers up and away from mouth

Synonyms—Yell, scream

SHOW

Touch index finger to left palm and bring hands forward

Synonym—Demonstrate

SHY

Place back of fingers against cheek, fingertips pointing to ear; move hand forward while raising fingertips

SICK
Touch right middle finger to forehead and left middle finger to stomach

Synonym—Ill

SIGN
Alternately rotate index fingers in toward self

Synonym—Sign language

SILLY
Stretch thumb and small finger; touch thumb to nose and flick hand down

SIMILAR
"Y" handshape moves from side to side

Synonyms—Too, also

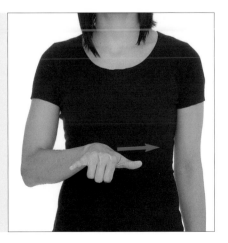 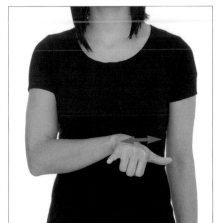

SIMPLE
Bring thumb and index finger together on each hand; strike right fingers down past same fingers of left hand

SINCE
Point index fingers back over right shoulder; bring fingers forward

SISTER
Extend index fingers and thumbs; lower right thumb from chin to rest right hand on left

SIT
Hook index and middle finger and lower onto same fingers of left hand

 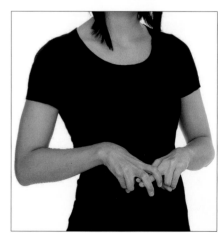

SITUATION

Point index finger up; rotate
right fist around finger

SIX

With palm facing out, bring tips of small finger and
thumb together, other fingers raised

SKEPTICAL

Crook index and middle fingers
in front of eyes twice

SKI

Hook index fingers up; move
both hands forward twice

SKILL

Clasp edge of left palm;
pull clasping hand out to
"A" handshape

SKIN

Pinch cheek with thumb and crooked
forefinger; shake slightly

SLEEP

Bring open hand down past
face and close fingers

SLEEPY

Cup both hands, palms in; bring
right hand down from eyebrows
and close to left hand twice

SLOW
Place right hand on back of left hand, palms down, and slide slowly up forearm

 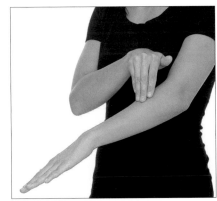

SMALL
Bring palms close together twice

Synonym—Little

SMART
Touch forehead with index finger; raise finger up and forward

Synonym—Intelligent

SMELL
Skim nose with inside of fingers twice using small forward circular motions

SMILE
Touch fingers to either side of mouth; tilt hands up and smile

Synonym—Grin

SMOOTH
Rest fingertips of each hand on thumbs; move hands forward while sliding fingers into "A" handshapes

SNOW
Spread fingers, with palms out, hands either side of head; bring hands down while wiggling fingers

SOAP
Brush in tips of fingers on palm twice

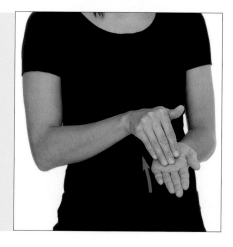

SOCCER

Using chopping motion, raise hand to strike edge of other hand twice at right angles

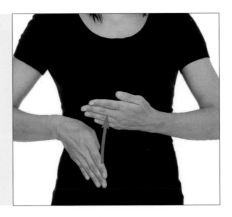 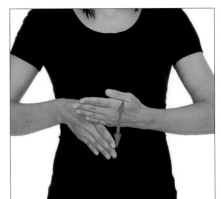

SOCKS

Bring index fingers together, both pointing down; alternately slide fingers up and down each other

 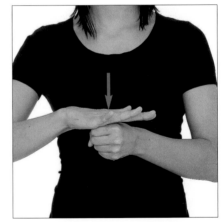

SODA

Dip middle finger into other clenched fist; remove middle finger and bring palm down on fist

SOFT

Lower open hands twice, closing hands on each downward movement

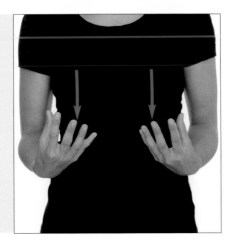 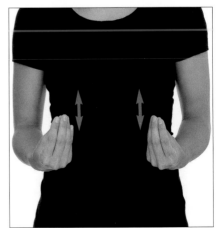

259

SOMETHING

Raise index finger and rotate hand from elbow using small inward circular motions, keeping hand and finger vertical

Synonym—Someone

SOMETIMES

Flick index finger up from left palm twice

Synonym—Occasionally

SON

Side of right hand moves from forehead down to rest on left forearm

SOON

Bring index finger and thumb together and tap chin twice

SORRY

Rotate "A" handshape
twice against chest

Synonyms—Apologize, regret

SO-SO

With palm down and fingers
stretched out, rock hand
from side to side a few times

**Synonyms—Sort of, more or less,
OK, average, fair, indifferent,
mediocre, middling**

SOUTH

Bring fist down

SPAGHETTI

Point little fingers toward each other;
circle hands toward each other,
then out and around again

SPECIAL

Grab left index finger between right thumb and index finger and lift

SPIDER

Cross right wrist down over left, fingers clawed; wiggle fingers while moving hands forward

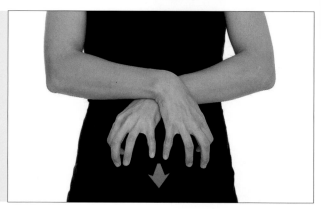

SQUIRREL

Crook index and middle fingers; bring hands together and away twice so that fingernails touch

STAIRS

Crook index and middle fingers; raise hand diagonally while making fingers "walk" up stairs

STAND

"Stand" index and middle fingers on left palm

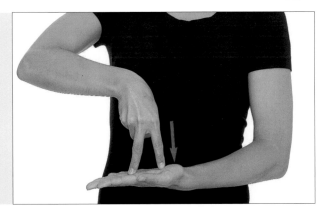

START

Twist index finger between index and middle finger of left hand as hands move down

Synonym—Begin

STAY

Stretch thumbs and small fingers out so that thumbs meet in middle; bring right hand down

Synonym—Remain

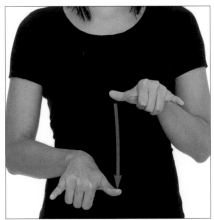

STEAL

Touch left elbow with index and middle finger of right hand; crook fingers and bring hand out and down

STILL (CONTINUING)

Stretch thumbs and small fingers out; smoothly move hands down, forward, and up

STOP

Bring edge of right hand down onto left palm

Synonym—Cease

STORE

Bring fingers together at either side of chest; swivel hands forward twice at wrists

STORY (TALE)

Fingers together and thumbs apart; hands join at 90 degrees, close and separate; open, twist, meet, close, and separate again

STRANGE

Cup hand, thumb beside cheek;
sweep hand down in front of face

Synonyms—Weird, peculiar

STRICT

Crook index and middle
fingers; raise hand so that
index finger rests on nose

STUBBORN

Touch thumb on side of head,
fingers upright; flap fingers
forward and down to palm

STUCK

Bring index and middle
fingers up to touch throat

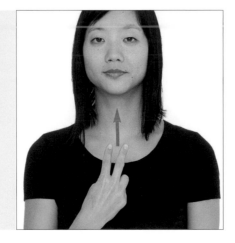 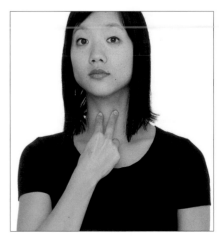

STUCK UP
Touch tip of index finger to nose and push head slightly back

Synonym—Snob

STUDENT
Place outstretched fingertips on left palm; lift hand, bringing fingers together, then drop and open fingers

STUDY
Use fingertips to tap left palm twice

STUPID
Bring back of index and middle fingers up to rest on forehead

Synonym—Ignorant

SUBTRACT

Close open hand into fist on left palm; move away, drop, and open

Synonym—Minus

SUCCEED

Touch index fingers to either side of chin; bring hands out and sweep up to vertical

Synonym—Finally

SUFFER

Touch thumb to chin and twist twice

SUMMARIZE

Open hands and stretch fingers, palms in; bring hands together as fists, right on top of left

Synonym—Condense

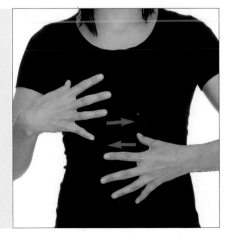
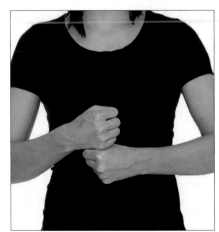

SUMMER
Lay index finger horizontally on forehead; pull finger across head while crooking finger

SUN
Cup hand around eye; move hand out and up

SUNDAY
Palms out; rotate hands using outward circular motions

SUNRISE
Fold arms in front of chest; raise cupped right hand up over left arm

Synonym—Dawn

SUNSET
Lower cupped right hand
down past left arm

Synonym—Twilight

SUPERVISE
Make "V" handshapes, right resting on left; move
hands together in two horizontal circles

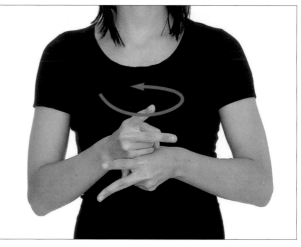

Synonyms—Manage, take care of

SUPPORT
Right fist pushes left fist up

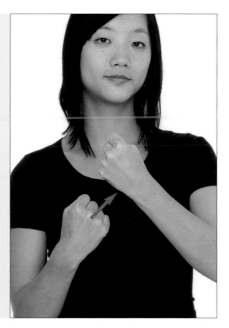

SUSPICIOUS
Index finger touches forehead above right eye, then moves out to crook. Repeat motion

SWALLOW
Touch index finger to chin and slide finger down throat

SWEET
Swipe fingertips down across chin twice

SWEETHEART
Bring knuckles together; fold
and unfold thumbs twice

From Table to Two

TABLE
Right arm bounces twice on left

TAKE
Palm down, fingers outstretched; bring hand toward self while clenching fist

TAKE IT EASY
Hands outstretched, fingers pointing out; bob hands from side to side and up and down

Synonym—Relax

TALK
Tip of "4" handshape taps
chin twice

Synonym—Speak

TALL
Slide index finger up left palm

TEA
Index finger and thumb together,
dip twice in cupped left hand

TEACH
"O" handshapes move forward
and down twice from forehead

TEAM
"T" handshape thumbs meet, then hands move out and back together while turning around

TEASE
Hook index fingers; rub one hand out over the other and repeat

TELEPHONE
Bounce thumb and little finger handshape twice on side of face

TELL
Touch tip of index finger to chin; bring hand forward and down

TEMPERATURE
Slide side of horizontal index finger up and down side of left vertical index finger twice

TEMPTED
Crook index finger and tap left elbow twice

TEN
Thumb up, knuckles forward; shake hand from side to side

TEND TO
Both hands have middle fingers bent in; right hand middle finger touches chest near heart and left hand is in front to the left; both hands move forward and down

TERRIBLE

Bring index finger and thumb together on both hands; flick fingers open

Synonym—Horrible

TEST

Point index fingers up at shoulder level; lower hands while crooking fingers, then spread fingers down

Synonym—Exam

THAN

Fold fingers in on both hands; swipe right hand down so that fingertips slap left fingertips

THANK YOU

Hand moves forward and down from chin

THANKSGIVING

Point index finger and thumb down from chin and move hand down to chest

THAT

Move thumb and small finger handshape down onto left palm

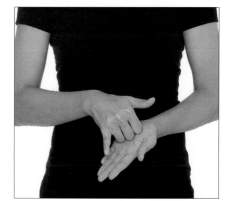

THEIR

Palm sweeps around in an arc

THEY

Index finger sweeps around in an arc

Synonyms—Those, these

THICK
Make hand a wide claw shape
and bring fingertips to cheek

THIN
Thumb and index finger move
down body past face

Synonym—Slim

THING
Slightly cup hand, palm up;
bounce twice to the right

THINK
Touch index finger to side of head

THIRSTY
Slide index finger along throat, top to bottom

THREE
Extend thumb, index, and middle fingers, palm in

THRILLED
Touch middle fingers to either side of chest; briskly flick hands apart and up

Synonym—Excited

THROUGH
Slide edge of hand through and between index and middle finger of left hand

THROW AWAY

Flick index and middle fingers out
straight from the fist

THUNDER

Touch ear with index finger,
then alternately rock fists in
and out at chest level

Synonym—Loud

THURSDAY

Handshape moves
from "T" to "H"

TICKET

Crooked index and middle
fingers of left hand punch
edge of left hand twice

TIGER

Claw hands move out across cheeks twice

TIME

Crooked index finger moves down back of other wrist

TIRED

Touch bent fingers to either side of chest, thumbs up; twist hands down from fingertips

Synonym—Weary

TODAY

"Y" handshapes move down; right arm with index finger extended moves down onto left arm

TOMORROW
Thumb touches right side of cheek and swings forward

TOUCH
Middle finger taps back of left hand

TRAIN (LOCOMOTIVE)
Slide index and middle finger up and down back of same fingers on left hand twice

TRASH
Tap palm twice against side of head

TRAVEL

Crook index and middle fingers; rotate hand in small counterclockwise horizontal circles while moving up and to the left

Synonym—Trip

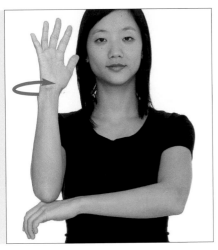

TREE

With right elbow resting on back of left hand, spread fingers and waggle right hand

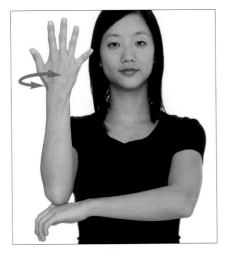

TRUST

Stretch fingers, left hand above the right, palms in; curl fingers to form fists and move hands down

TRY

"A" handshapes at chest
swivel down and forward

Synonym—Attempt

TUESDAY

"T" handshape rotates with small
outward circular motions

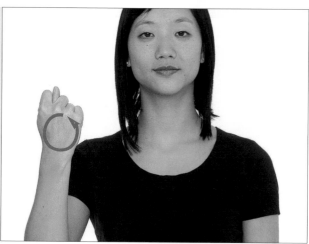

TURTLE

Place left hand over right fist;
raise and lower right thumb

TWO

With palm in, index and
middle finger form "V"

UGLY

Place index finger beneath nose; move hand away to side while bending finger

UMBRELLA

Place right fist on top of left; raise right hand and bring back down to left hand

UNCLE

"U" handshape moves in two small circles at side of head

UNDER

Right fist, with thumb extended, moves down and below left palm

Synonym—Below

UNDERSTAND

Snap finger up from fist next to head

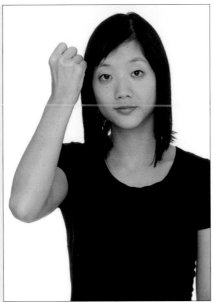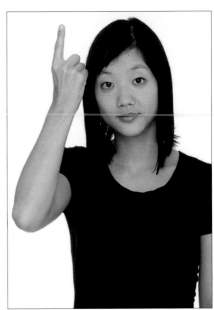

UNTIL
Bring tip of right index
finger down to touch
tip of left index finger

Synonym—To

UPSET
Place palm on stomach
and flip over

USE
Make two circles with "U"
handshape on back of left fist

Synonym—Wear

VACATION
Fingers stretched, touch thumbs to either side of chest twice

VAGUE
Fingers stretched, rub palms together using a circular motion

VISIT
"V" handshapes rotate alternately using an outward circular motion

From Wait to Wrong

WAIT

Raise both hands to left side, palms facing up;
move hands in small forward circles while
wiggling fingers

WAKE UP

Thumbs and index fingers
separate at sides of face near eyes

Synonym—Surprised

WALK

Hands alternately rock back and
forth as do feet when walking

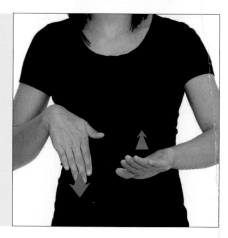

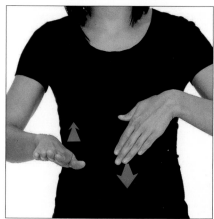

WANT
Move claw hands in toward
body while crooking
all ten fingers

WARM
Move closed hand fingertips
out from mouth while
opening fingers

WARN
Tap back of hand twice

WASH
Bring knuckles together;
scrub top hand back and
forward over left hand a
few times

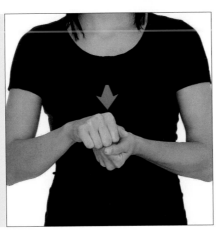 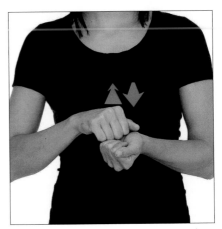

WATER
Tap chin twice with index finger of "W" handshape

WE
Touch index finger to right side of chest then the left

Synonym—Us

WEAK
Touch tips of spread fingers to left palm; bend and unbend fingertips into palm twice

WEDNESDAY
Rotate "W" handshape from elbow using inward circular motions

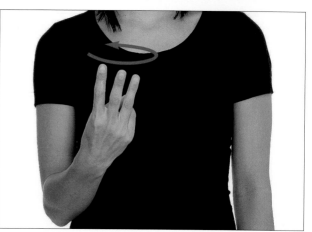

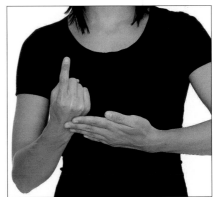

WEEK
Raise index finger and slide back of hand out along left palm

WEIGH
Place index and middle finger across same fingers of left hand; tilt top fingers backward and forward twice

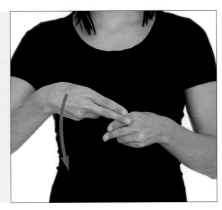
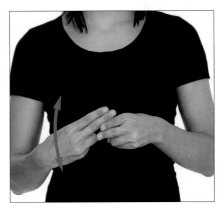

WEST
"W" handshape moves across body to the left

WET
Touch chin with index finger; bring both hands in front of chest, palms in, fingers up, and close fingers twice

293

WHAT?
Open hands and stretch fingers, palms up; move hands back and forth

WHAT'S UP?
Touch chest with middle finger; flick hand out so finger points up

Synonym—How are you?

WHEN?
Right index finger circles clockwise down onto left index finger

WHERE?
Wag index finger two or three times

WHICH?
Thumbs up, back of hands facing out; alternately move hands up and down

WHITE
Place open fingertips on chest; take hand away while bringing fingertips together

WHO?
Touch thumb tip of "L" handshape on chin; crook index finger twice

WHY?
Touch ring, middle, and index finger to side of head; bring hand down to "Y" handshape

WIFE

Touch thumb tip of cupped right hand to right side of chin; bring hand down to clasp left hand

WILL

Move hand forward from side of head

WILLING

Palm turns over, forward and down from chest

WIN

Right claw hand mimes grabbing something from left fist and moves up

WINDOW

Palms in, bring edge of right hand down onto left hand and repeat

WINE

Rotate "W" handshape in small forward circles at cheek

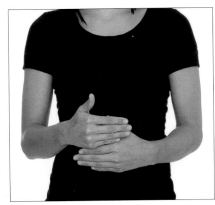

WINTER

Fists move in small outward circles

WISH

Cupped hand slides down chest

WITH
"A" handshapes move together once

WITHOUT
Make the sign WITH, then separate hands while spreading fingers

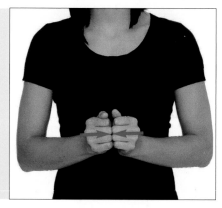 

WOMAN
Thumb of open hand moves from chin down to chest

WONDERFUL
Palms out, move hands forward, back and forward again

Synonyms—Great, fantastic

WOOD
Use edge of hand to mime sawing on back of other hand

WORD
Tap extended thumb and index finger twice on left index finger

WORK
Tap right wrist twice down onto back of left wrist

Synonym—Job

WORLD
Right "W" handshape circles outward around left "W" and comes to rest on it

WORRY
Fold in thumbs and alternately rotate hands in toward face

 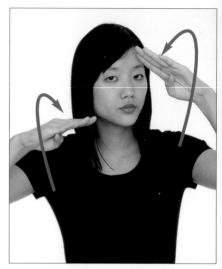

WORSE
"V" handshapes cross each other, right over left

Synonym—Multiply

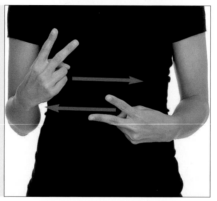 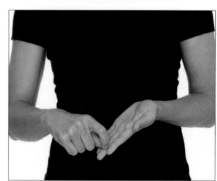

WRITE
Bend thumb and index finger together; drag across left palm

 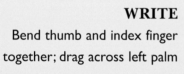

WRONG
Stretch thumb and small finger; bring knuckles to touch chin

From Year to Your

YEAR
Right fist circles forward around left fist and comes to rest on top

YELLOW
"Y" handshape swivels back and forth near right shoulder

YES
Bend fist down twice

YESTERDAY
Extended thumb touches jaw
near chin and moves back

YOU
Point index finger out

YOUNG
Fingers touch chest near
shoulders and flick up twice

YOUR
Palm out, push hand forward

Index

Main entries are in plain text, synonyms are listed in bold.

abandon 14
about 14
about (roughly) 27
above 14
accept 15
acquire 125
act 15
add to 15
address 15
advertise 16
advise 16
afford 211
afraid 16
Africa 16
after 17
afternoon 17
again 17
against 17
agitated 149
agony 131
agree 18
ahead 18
air conditioner 18
airplane 19
alarm 19
alcohol 19
all 19
all over 20
all right 20
allergy 20
alligator 21
allow 21
almost 21
alone 21
already 113
also 253
alternate 22
always 22
amazed 22
ambulance 22
America 23
analyze 23
and 23
angry 23
announce 24
another 209
answer 24
anxious 24
any 24
anyone 25
anyway 25
apologize 261
apparently 248
appear (show up) 25
applaud 25
apple 26
apply 26
appointment 26
appreciate 99
appropriate 241
approve 26
approximately 27
area 27
argue 232
arrest 27
arrive 27
art 28
article 28
artificial 28
ashamed 28
ask 29
assign 29
assistant 29
associate with 29
attempt 284
attend 30
attitude 30
attracted to 30
audience 30
aunt 31
automobile 53
average 31
avoid 31
awful 174
awkward 31

baby 32
bad 32
bake 32
balance 33
banana 33
barely 33
baseball 33
basement 34
basic 34
basketball 34
bathroom 239
bear (animal) 35
beat 79
beautiful 227
because 35
become 35
bed 35
bee 190
beer 36
before 36
beg 36
begin 263
believe 37
bell 37
below 37
benefit 37
best 38
bet 38
better 38
between 39
bicycle 39
big 39
biology 39
birth 43
birthday 40
black 40
blind 40
blouse 40
blow up (temper) 41
blue 41
boast 41
boat 41
body 42
boil (with anger) 42
book 42
boring 42
born 43
borrow 43
boss 43
both 43
bother 44
bowling 44
box 241
boy 44
bracelet 44
brag 41
brave 45
bread 45
break (damage) 45
breakfast 45
breathe 46
bridge 46
brief 251
bring 46
broke (no money) 46
brother 47
brown 47
bug (insect) 47
build 47
bulletin board 48
burn 113
burp 48
bury 48
busy 48
but 49
butter 49
butterfly 49
buy 49

California 50
call (summon) 50
camera 50
camp 51
can (able) 51
Canada 51
cancel 51
candle 52
candy 52
can't 52
captain 43
caption 52
car 53
careful 53
careful, be 53

careless 53
carry 46
cat 54
catch up 54
Catholic 54
cause (verb) 54
cautious 53
cease 264
celebrate 55
cellar 34
cent 55
center 185
certificate 55
chair 55
challenge 56
champion 56
change (modify) 56
character (personal) 57
charge 57
chase 57
chat 57
cheap 58
cheat 58
cheerful 58
cheese 58
chemistry 59
chicken 59
children 59
China 59
chocolate 60
choose 60
cigar 60
cigarette 60
city 61
class 61
clean (adjective) 61
clean up (verb) 61
clear 62
close (near) 195
close (verb) 62
closet 62
clothes 62
clouds 63
clumsy 31
coffee 63
cold (adjective) 63
cold (noun) 63
collect 92
college 64
color 64
comb 64
come 64
comfortable 65
command 65
communicate 65
commute 65
compare 66
compete 66
complain 66
complicated 66
compliment 25
computer 67
concerned 24
concerning 14
conceited 94
concentrate 215
concept 148
condense 267
conference 183
confident 45
confidential 247
conflict 67
confused 67
congratulate 67
connect 68
consider 223
contact 68
content 245
contented 136
continue 68
control 68
convince 69
cook 69
cookie 69
cool (good) 69
cool (temperature) 70
cooperate 70
copy 70
corn 70
corner 71
correct 241
cost 71
cough 71
counsel 16

country 71
cousin 72
cow 72
crave 72
crazy 73
create 73
credit card 57
criticize 73
crocodile 21
cross (verb) 74
crowded 74
cruel 180
cry 74
culture 75
curious 75
cute 75

damage 82
dance 76
dangerous 76
dare 56
dark 76
darn 77
daughter 77
dawn 268
day 77
dead 77
deaf 78
debate 85
debt 211
deceive 78
decide 78
decline 78
decrease 79
deep 79
defeat 79
defend 238
delete 79
delicious 80
delighted 94
demonstrate 252
demoted 80
deodorant 80
depart 81
depend on 81
depressed 81
describe 105
desire 72
desperate 81
destroy 82
deteriorate 82
devil 82
dictionary 83
die 77
different 83
difficult 83
dinner 83
diploma 84
dirty 84
disagree 84
disappear 84
disappointed 187
disconnect 85
discover 112
discuss 85
dislike 87
dissolve 183
distant 108
distribute 85
divide (math) 85
divorce 86
doctor 86
doesn't matter 86
dog 86
dollar 87
don't 201
don't care 87
don't know 87
don't like 87
don't mind 88
don't want 88
door 88
doubt (unsure) 89
drama 15
dream 89
drink 89
drive car 90
drop 90
drown 90
drug store 90
during 91
Dutch, Go 91
duty 91

each 92
eager 99
early 92
earn 92
earrings 93
Earth 93
East 93
easy 93
eat 94
eavesdrop 210
ecstatic 94
edgy 149
egg 94
egotistical 94
eight 95
either 95
election 95
electricity 95
elephant 96
elevator 96
embarrassed 96
emergency 97
emotional 97
empty 97
encourage 97
end 98
engaged (betrothed) 98
England 98
English 98
enjoy 99
enough 99
enter 99
enthusiastic 99
equal 100
error 187
escape 100
establish 100
Europe 101
evening 199
every 92
everywhere 20
exact 101
exaggerate 101
exam 276
excited 102
excuse 102
excuse me 102
exercise (physical) 103
expand 103
expect 103
expensive 104
experience 104
expert 104
explain 105
express 105
eyes 105

face 106
factory 176
fail 106
faint 106
fair 100, 261
fake 227
fall asleep 107
fall behind 107
fall down 107
fall in love 107
family 108
famous 108
fantastic 298
fantasy 108
far 108
farm 109
fascinated 30
fast 109
fat 109
father 109
fault 110
favorite 110
fearful 16
fed up 110
feed 111
feel 111
female 126
fence 111
few 111
fight 112
figure out 112
fill 123
finally 267
find 112
fine 113
finish 113
fire (flame) 113

fire (from job) 113
first 114
fish 114
fishing 114
five 115
fix 115
flag 115
flatter 116
flexible 116
flirt 116
flower 117
follow (trail) 117
football 117
for 118
forbidden 118
force 118
foreign 118
forever 119
forgive 102
forget 119
fork 119
former 36, 214
fortunate 175
four 119
France 120
French 120
free 120
freeze 120
french fries 121
frequently 205
Friday 121
friendly 58
from 121
front 122
frustrated 122
full 123
fun 123
funny 123
future 123

Gallaudet 124
game 124
garage 124
general 125
generous 159
gentle 159
German 125
Germany 125
get (acquire) 125
get in 125
get on 126
get up 126
giraffe 126
girl 126
give 127
give in 127
give up 14
glad 136
glass 127
go 127
Go Dutch 91
God 128
golf 128
good 128
gossip 129
government 129
graduate 129
grandfather 129
grandmother 130
great 298
greedy 130
green 130
grief 131
grin 258
group 131
grow 131
grow up 132
guarantee 229
guess 186
guilty 132
gullible 132
gun 133

habit 134
hair 134
hamburger 134
hands 135
handsome 135
hanger 135
happen 136
happy 136
harass 218
hard (difficult) 83

hard (solid) 136
hard of hearing 136
hat 137
hate 137
have 137
have to 193
he 137
head 138
healthy 45
hear 138
hearing aid 138
heart 139
heat 145
heaven 139
heavy 139
hell 139
hello 140
help 140
her 142
here 140
hide 141
high 141
high school 141
highway 141
hire 142
his 142
history 142
hockey 143
hold 143
holy 143
home 144
honest 144
honor 144
hope 103
horrible 276
horse 144
hospital 145
hot 145
hour 145
house 145
how 146
how are you? 294
however 49
how many 146
humble 146
humid 146
hungry 147
hurry 147
hurt 147
husband 147
hypocrite 227

I 148
ice cream 148
idea 148
if 149
ignorant 266
ignore 149
ill 253
illegal 118
impatient 149
important 150
impossible 150
improve 150
in 150
include 151
incompetent 151
increase 151
India 151
indifferent 261
individual 152
influence 152
inform 152
injure 147
innocent 153
inquire 29
insane 73
insect 47
inspired 153
insult 153
intelligent 257
interesting 154
intermission 154
interrupt 154
interview 155
introduce 155
invent 73
invite 142
Ireland 155
it 137
Italy 155

jail 156
Japan 156

Japanese 156
jealous 156
Jewish 157
job 299
join 213
jump 157

keep 158
keep (save) 246
key 158
kick 159
kill 159
kind 159
kiss 160
kitchen 160
kneel 160
knife 161
know 161

lamp 162
language 162
large 39
last (final) 163
late (not on time) 163
lately 235
later 163
laugh 164
law 164
lazy 164
lead (guide) 165
learn 165
leave (behind) 165
leave (depart) 81
lecture 166
lend 43
less than 37
lesson 166
letter 166
liberal 208
library 167
license 167
lie 167
lie down 168
life 171
light 162
light (weight) 168
lighthearted 136
lightning 168
like 169
limit 169
line of work 169
liquor 19
list (noun) 170
listen 170
little 257
little bit 170
live 171
locked 171
London 171
lonely 172
long 172
look at 172
look for 173
Los Angeles 173
lose (competition) 173
lose (misplace) 174
loud 280
lousy 174
love 174
low 175
lucky 175
luggage 175
lunch 175

machine 176
mad (with rage) 23
magazine 176
magic 177
mail 166
major (academic) 169
make (produce) 177
male 44
man 177
manage 68, 269
many 178
march 178
marry 178
match (fire) 179
match (fit) 179
math 179
maximum 180
maybe 180
me 148
mean (nasty) 180

meaning 181
measure 181
meat 181
mechanic 182
medicine 182
mediocre 261
medium 31
meet 182
meeting 183
melt 183
memorize 183
Mexico 184
microscope 184
microwave oven 184
middle 185
middling 261
military 185
milk 185
mingle 29
minimum 186
minus 267
minute 186
mischievous 82
misery 131
miss (don't notice) 211
miss (fail to catch) 186
miss (wish to see) 187
mistake 187
mock (ridicule) 187
modest 146
modify 56
Monday 188
money 188
month 188
moon 189
more 189
more or less 261
morning 189
mosquito 190
most 190
mother 190
motor 176
motorcycle 191
mountain 191
mouse 191
move (from/to) 192
movie 192
multiply 300
music 192
must 193
my 193
myself 193

naive 132
name 194
napkin 194
nasty 180
nation 71
near 195
nearly 21
neat (tidy) 61
neat (good) 195
negative (adjective) 195
neglect 149
neighbor 198
nephew 196
nervous 196
never 196
new 197
New York 197
newspaper 197
next (in order) 198
next (to) 198
nice 198
niece 199
night 199
nine 199
no 200
none 200
North 200
nosey 201
not 201
not yet 201
nothing 202
notice 202
now 202
number 203
nurse 203

obtain 125
obvious 62
occasionally 260
occur 136
occur (to) 204

of course 204
offend 153
offer 205
often 205
oh, I see 205
okay 20, 113, 261
old 206
once 206
one 206
onion 207
only 207
open 207
open minded 208
opinion 208
opportunity 208
oppose 17
opposite 209
orange 209
order 65
organize 221
other 209
ought to 252
our 210
out 210
overhear 210
overlook 211
owe 211
own 137

paint 212
paper 212
parade 178
Paris 213
parking 213
participate 213
party 214
pass 214
past 214
patient (adjective) 215
pay 215
pay attention 215
payable 211
peace 216
peculiar 265
people 216
perfect 216
perform 15
permit 21
person 217
personality 217
persuade 69
philosophy 217
photocopy 218
photograph 219
physics 218
pick on 218
picnic 245
picture 219
pie 219
pink 219
pity 220
pizza 220
place (location) 220
plan 221
plant 221
play 221
play (theater) 15
plead 36
pleasant 58
please 222
pleased 136
plumber 182
police 222
polite 222
politics 223
ponder 223
poor 223
popcorn 224
popular 224
positive 224
possess 137
possible 225
powerful 225
practice (rehearse) 225
pray 226
predict 226
prefer 226
pregnant 226
president 227
pretend 227
pretty 227
prevent 227
previous 214

price 71
.prison 156
private 247
probably 180
problem 228
proceed 228
process 228
procure 125
profession 169
profit 228
promise 229
promoted 229
proper 241
Protestant 229
proud 229
prove 230
punish 230
purple 230
put 231
puzzled 231

quarrel 232
question 29
quick 109
quiet 232
quit 233

rabbit 234
race 66
rage 41
rain 234
read 234
ready 235
real 235
realize 204
really 235
reason 235
receive 125
recently 235
recognize 202
red 236
reduce 236
refuse 236
regret 261
regular 236
reject 237
relax 239, 272
relieved 237
religion 237
rely on 81
remain 263
remember 237
repair 115
repeat 17
reply 24
rescue 244
resent 238
reservation 26
resign 238
resign (quit) 233
resist 238
respond 24
responsibility 238
rest 239
restaurant 239
restless 149
restroom 239
retire (from work) 239
revenge 240
rich 240
ride in 240
ride on 240
ridicule 187
right (correct) 241
right (entitlement) 241
river 241
room 241
roommate 242
rough 242
rude 242
ruin 242
rule (policy) 243
rumor 129
run (exercise) 243
rural 71
rush 147
Russia 243

sad 244
safe (protected) 244
same 244
San Francisco 245
sandwich 245
satisfied 245

Saturday 245
save (keep) 246
save (rescue) 244
say 246
scared 16
school 246
science 246
scold 247
scream 252
search 173
secret 247
secretary 247
see 247
seem 248
selfish 248
semester 248
send 248
sensitive 249
sentence 249
separate 249
serious 249
seven 250
several 250
she 137
ship 41
shirt 250
shocked 250
shoes 251
shopping 251
short (height) 251
short (time) 251
should 252
shout 252
show 252
show (theater) 15
shy 252
sick 253
sign 253
sign language 253
silly 253
similar 253
simple 254
since 254
single 21
sister 254
sit 254
situation 255
six 255
skeptical 255
ski 255
skill 256
skin 256
sleep 256
sleepy 256
slim 278
slow 257
small 257
smart 257
smell 257
smile 258
smooth 258
snob 266
snow 258
soap 258
soccer 259
socks 259
soda 259
soft 259
solid 136
someone 260
something 260
sometimes 260
son 260
soon 260
sorry 261
sort of 261
so-so 261
South 261
spaghetti 261
speak 273
special 262
speech 166
spider 262
spoil 242
sports 124
spring (season) 221
squirrel 262
stairs 262
stand 263
start 263
stay 263
steal 263
still (continuing) 264
stop 264

store 264
story (tale) 264
strange 265
strict 265
strong 225
stubborn 265
stuck 265
stuck up 266
student 266
study 266
stupid 266
subtract 267
succeed 267
suffer 267
suggest 205
suitcase 175
summarize 267
summer 268
summon 50
sun 268
Sunday 268
sunrise 268
sunset 269
superintendent 227
supervise 269
support 269
sure 235
surprised 22, 290
surrender 14
suspicious 270
swallow 270
sweet 270
sweetheart 271
sympathy 220

table 272
take 272
take care of 269
take it easy 272
talk 273
tall 273
tea 273
teach 273
team 274
tease 274
telephone 274
tell 274
temperature 275
tempted 275
ten 275
tend to 275
tendency 134
terrible 276
test 276
than 276
thank you 276
thanksgiving 277
that 277
theater 15
their 277
there 137
these 277
they 277
thick 278
thin 278
thing 278
think 278
thirsty 279
those 277
three 279
thrilled 279
through 279
throw away 280
thunder 280
Thursday 280
ticket 280
tiger 281
time 281
tired 281
to 288
today 281
toilet 239
tomorrow 282
too 253
touch 282
town 61
tolerant 215
train (locomotive) 282
train (practice) 225
trash 282
travel 283
tree 283
trick 78
trip 283

true 235
trust 283
truth 144
try 284
Tuesday 284
turtle 284
twilight 269
two 285
typical 236

ugly 286
umbrella 286
unable 52
uncle 287
under 287
understand 287
unfortunately 77
unpaid 211
until 288
upset 288
us 292
use 288
usual 236

vacation 289
vague 289
video 192
visit 289

wait 290
wake up 290
walk 290
want 291
warm 291
warn 291
wash 291
watch 172
water 292
we 292
weak 292
wealthy 240
wear 288
weary 281
Wednesday 292
week 293
weigh 293
weird 265
West 293
wet 293
what? 294
what's up? 294
when? 294
where? 294
which? 295
while 91
white 295
who? 295
why? 295
wife 296
will 296
willing 296
win 296
window 297
wine 297
winter 297
wish 297
with 298
without 298
withstand 238
woman 298
wonderful 298
wood 299
word 299
work 299
world 299
worried 24
worry 300
worse 300
write 300
wrong 300

Xerox 218

year 301
yell 252
yellow 301
yes 301
yesterday 302
you 302
young 302
your 302